# *The* POPULAR BIBLE PROPHECY WORKBOOK

## TIM LaHAYE & ED HINDSON

HARVEST HOUSE PUBLISHERS

EUGENE, OREGON

*Cover Design by Terry Dugan Design, Minneapolis, Minnesota*

**THE POPULAR BIBLE PROPHECY WORKBOOK**
Copyright © 2006 by Pre-Trib Research Center, Tim LaHaye, and Ed Hindson
Published by Harvest House Publishers
Eugene, Oregon 97402
www.harvesthousepublishers.com

ISBN-13: 978-0-7369-1694-3
ISBN-10: 0-7369-1694-6

**Printed in the United States of America**

06  07  08  09  10  11  12  13  14 / ML-MS / 10  9  8  7  6  5  4  3  2  1

# CONTENTS

# WHAT DOES THE FUTURE HOLD?

Everyone is curious about the future. We all want to know what is going to happen next. But only God has the ability to see what is to come. Therefore, we must rely on His Word as our guide to understanding what lies ahead.

We are living in incredible times. Things are changing so fast we can hardly keep up with them. Before we can catch our breath, we are hurried on to the next significant event on the horizon. Tensions in the Middle East, the development of weapons of mass destruction, and threats to global peace fill the newspaper headlines. We all sense that the world is moving toward some great climax.

People today are asking, Where are we headed? What will happen next? And how can we be prepared? These are the very questions that Bible prophecy answers for us. Prophecy helps us to see into the future with clarity and confidence.

The purpose of Bible prophecy is not to frighten us, but to assure us that God is in control. In times of human uncertainty, we can rest assured that we have "a sure word of prophecy" that shines like a beacon of light into the darkness of our times. Therefore, we can lift our heads and "look up," knowing that our redemption is drawing near (Luke 21:28).

The purpose of this study is to help us examine what the Bible says about the future. We will look at key Bible prophecies about such matters as the rapture of the church and the rise of the Antichrist. We will explore major prophetic passages that describe the Tribulation, Christ's glorious appearing, the millennial kingdom, and heaven.

The hope of the second coming of Christ is a strong encouragement for us to live right. The Bible reminds us, "Abide in Him, that when He appears, we may have confidence and not be ashamed before Him at His coming. . . . we know that when He is revealed, we shall be like Him, for we shall see Him as He is. And everyone who has this hope in Him purifies Himself, just as He is pure" (1 John 2:28; 3:2-3).

God bless you as you study these great prophetic truths. May they challenge your mind, move your heart, and lift your soul with great anticipation for the Savior's return.

Tim LaHaye

Ed Hindson

# 1
# ONLY GOD CAN PROPHESY

The uniqueness of God is expressed in the predictive nature of Bible prophecy. There is nothing like this in any other religion. Only the God of the Bible can predict the future with perfect accuracy. "For I am God, and there is no other... declaring the end from the beginning, and from ancient times things that are not yet done.... Indeed I have spoken it; I will also bring it to pass" (Isaiah 46:9-11).

Jesus Christ also claimed divine authority for the prophetic Scriptures. The most dramatic prophecies in all the Bible point to the coming Messiah-Savior who would both suffer and reign. These ancient prophecies were so precisely fulfilled that there can be no serious doubt that they point to only one person who has ever lived—Jesus of Nazareth.

After His resurrection, Jesus told His disciples, "All things must be fulfilled which were written in the Law of Moses and the Prophets and the Psalms concerning Me" (Luke 24:44). Christ Himself then taught the disciples which Old Testament scriptures predicted His life and ministry. "He opened their understanding that they might comprehend the Scriptures" (verse 45).

The New Testament writers were instructed by the Lord Himself regarding biblical prophecies and their fulfillment. The threefold designation—law, prophets, and psalms—refers to the three major divisions of the Hebrew Bible. Jesus was specifically stating that the entire Old Testament (law, prophets, psalms) predicted the details of His life, ministry, death, and resurrection. Therefore, the preaching of the early Christian disciples was filled with references to Old Testament prophecies and their fulfillment in the person of Jesus Christ (see Acts 2:25-36; 3:22-23; 4:25-26; 13:46-49).

During His earthly ministry, Jesus was recognized as a "prophet" of God (Matthew 21:11; Luke 7:16) and a "teacher" from God (John 3:2). Jesus even referred to Himself as a "prophet" (Matthew 13:57; Luke 13:33). The early preaching of the apostles also emphasized the prophetic nature of Christ's ministry (Acts 3:24-26; 7:37). Matthew's gospel alone makes 65 references to Old Testament scriptures, emphasizing their fulfillment in Christ.

## The Prophet and the Prophetic Ministry

The prophetical histories are followed in the Hebrew canon by the prophetical books of prediction. The two form a unit in the middle portion of the threefold canon, under the common term "prophets." They are distinguished as the "former prophets" and "latter prophets." The manner of speaking by the prophets may be best characterized as preaching. Their messages also included symbolic actions (2 Kings 13:17-19), object lessons (Jeremiah 1:11-14), and written sermons (Jeremiah 36:4).

The Hebrew prophets were men of God who preached God's Word and also predicted the future. Their messages revealed events that were yet to come. In this regard, their messages were supernatural, not natural. They were derived neither from observation nor intellectual thought, but from knowing God and speaking with Him.

The revelation of God to the prophet is a process by which God reveals His secrets to the prophet (Amos 3:7). The term "reveal" (Hebrew, galah) means to "uncover," as in "uncovering the ear" (1 Samuel 9:15). Thus, when God "uncovers" the prophet's ear, He reveals what has been previously hidden (such as in 2 Samuel 7:27) so that the prophet "perceives" what the Lord has said (Jeremiah 23:18).

It is obvious, therefore, that the Spirit of God is necessary for prophetic inspiration. Thus, it was by the Spirit that the Word of the Lord was communicated to the prophet and by the Spirit that the Word was mediated to the people.

## Messianic Prophecy

The high aspirations of the Old Testament writers and their application of Godlike characteristics to a coming prince, the Messiah, the son of David, compel us to see one who is more than a mere man. He was called both the son of David and the Son of God.

The New Testament based its entire apologetic on the fact that Jesus was the Messiah predicted in the Old Testament, and that these predictions were conclusively fulfilled in Jesus' life. The New Testament recognizes the value of using predictive prophecy and its fulfillment as apologetical evidence to prove the supernaturalness and credibility of Christianity.

Jesus Himself was always aware that these prophecies "must be fulfilled." He subjected Himself completely to the course that they charted, under God's direction, and considered the details of His life and death as events that must take place because they were written in the Word of God. The purpose of messianic prophecy was to make the Messiah known after He had fulfilled the event foretold. These prophecies served as preparatory devices that signaled His arrival.

The New Testament writers insisted that Jesus was the Christ on the basis of three essential arguments:

1. Jesus' resurrection
2. Their eyewitness accounts of what happened
3. Fulfillment of Old Testament prophecies

Within weeks of the resurrection, the early Christians were proclaiming the events in Jesus' life as fulfillment of specific prophecies. In the first Christian sermon, Peter announced, "This is what was spoken by the prophet Joel.... David says concerning him... [that] He would raise up the Christ to sit on his throne, he, foreseeing this, spoke concerning the resurrection of the Christ" (Acts 2:16,25,30).

In following this line of proof the apostles were doing what had been done by God's prophets for centuries. They were pointing to the fulfillment of prophecy as the ultimate proof of the truthfulness of God's Word. In so doing, they were urging their listeners to believe the whole message of the gospel of Jesus Christ.

## Prophecies Fulfilled in the Life of Christ

The Old Testament is filled with prophecies about the human race, the nation of Israel, and future events in general. And the most important prophecies are those that point to the coming of Christ. These are not merely isolated "proof texts"; the whole of the Old Testament points the way to a coming future Messiah.

Many of these predictions were recognized as messianic by the Jews, even before the time of Jesus. Here are ten examples:

| Prophecy | Subject | Fulfillment |
|---|---|---|
| Genesis 3:15 "her seed" | Seed of a woman | Galatians 4:4 "born of a woman" |
| Genesis 12:3 "all the families of the earth shall be blessed" | Descendent of Abraham | Matthew 1:1 "the Son of Abraham" |
| Genesis 49:10 "the scepter shall not depart from Judah" | Tribe of Judah | Luke 3:33 "the son of Judah" |
| Isaiah 9:6-7 "Upon the throne of David" | Heir of David | Luke 1:32 "the throne of his father David" |

| Prophecy | Subject | Fulfillment |
|---|---|---|
| Micah 5:2 "Bethlehem…shall come…Ruler in Israel" | Born in Bethlehem | Luke 2:4-7 "to the city of David, which is called Bethlehem…she brought forth her firstborn" |
| Isaiah 7:14 "The virgin shall conceive" | Born of a virgin | Matthew 1:23 "The virgin shall be with child" |
| Psalm 2:7 "You are My Son" | Declared the Son of God | Matthew 3:17 "This is My beloved Son" |
| Isaiah 53:3 "He is despised and rejected" | Rejected by His own | John 1:11 "His own did not receive him" |
| Psalm 41:9 "my own familiar friend…against me" | Betrayed by a friend | Matthew 26:50 "Friend, why have you come?" |
| Zechariah 12:10 "on Me whom they pierced" | Death by crucifixion | Matthew 27:23 "Let Him be crucified!" |

There are about 120 distinct prophecies of the first coming of Christ in the Old Testament. They are like pieces of a puzzle. Each presents a distinct element of the Savior's life and ministry, but the whole picture portrayed by these pieces can only be seen after their fulfillment. Not until Jesus came did these prophecies come into clear relation with one another. The chances of all these prophecies being fulfilled in the life of one man is one chance in 84 followed by 131 zeroes.

$$8.4 \times 10^{132}$$

These 120 prophecies of Christ's first coming are overwhelming evidence of the divine origin of Scripture, the messiahship of Jesus, and the truth of Christianity. When viewed as a whole, the collective impact of these prophecies and their fulfillment in the Gospels cannot be easily dismissed by unbelievers. Again, the mathematical possibility of all these predictions being fulfilled in one person is absolutely astounding.

## What About Future Prophecies?

The accurate fulfillment of the prophecies of Christ's first coming point us to the certainty the 300 prophecies of His second coming will also be fulfilled. Because the prophecies relating to Christ's first coming have had a literal fulfillment, we can confidently expect that the prophecies relating to His second coming will have an equally literal fulfillment.

While there is every reason to believe in the trustworthiness of the Bible's prophecies about the future, they can be accepted only by faith until the time of their fulfillment. And our faith in these prophecies is not based on some misplaced, pious hope. Rather, it is based on the literal fulfillment of prophecies from the past. This alone gives us great confidence that the prophecies not yet fulfilled will indeed come to pass.

The fact that Bible prophecies have always been fulfilled in an exact and detailed manner assures us that, in regard to prophecies not yet fulfilled, Christ will come again just as He said (John 14:1-3). We can look forward to the unfolding of the future because we know the future is under the sovereign control of God.

John's Gospel ends by reminding us that the "world itself could not contain" the books that could be written about Jesus Christ (John 21:25). But John himself, Jesus' personal disciple, states, "These are written that you may believe that Jesus is the Christ, the Son of God, and that believing you may have life in His name" (John 20:31).

While biblical prophecies and their literal fulfillment may fascinate our curiosity and challenge our minds, they are ultimately intended to bring us to a personal point of decision and faith as well. If the Bible predicted these things would happen and they actually did happen, then we must take Jesus' claims about Himself seriously. If He alone fulfilled these prophecies, then He alone is the Savior, the Son of God. If so, then He is King of kings and Lord of lords. And if He is, then He deserves our faith, our lives, and our complete devotion.

# Lesson 1

# **Only God Can Prophesy**

When it comes to predicting the future, mankind has a poor record. We simply have no way of knowing what's going to happen tomorrow, the next day, the next month, or the next year. By contrast, God knows the future, and reveals glimpses of it in the Bible. And so far, every single prediction that's been fulfilled has occurred exactly the way God said it would. He has never even been slightly wrong.

1.  Read Isaiah 46:9-10. What is God able to do that no one else can do? *Tell what happens even before it happens*

2.  Read Isaiah 45:5-7. What things does the Lord do? What does this tell you about Him? *creates light & darkness, prepares us for battle, sends good & bad times. Sovereign*

3.  Read Psalm 33:10-11. What does this passage say about the plans of people? What does it say about the plans of the Lord? *He frustrates others. Stand firm Forever*

4.  What does Proverbs 21:1 tell us about God? *directs & guides our hearts*

5.  Based on the aforementioned Bible verses, how much control would you say God has over world events? *complete*

6.  What does this knowledge do to your level of confidence in God's ability to fulfill all the predictions He made in the Bible? *make it concrete.*

## *Applying Prophecy to Everyday Life*

Not only is God able to fulfill all the predictions in the Bible, but He's also able to keep all His promises. How does that benefit you as a Christian? *We can trust in God's word*

# 2
# UNDERSTANDING BIBLE PROPHECY

Finding your way through the maze of traffic in a major city can be difficult—especially if you don't know where you are going. Some people view Bible prophecy the same way. It looks like a hopeless maze of confusion about the future, so they throw up their hands in defeat. "I just can't make any sense out of this!" they exclaim in frustration.

One of the most difficult tasks in interpreting God's Word has been that of understanding the prophecies about the end times. First, we must remember that the people of Jesus' day missed many of the predictions of His first coming. Therefore, we must not presume that we have figured out all the details of His second coming. Second, we must guard against the great temptation to read prophecy through the eyes of the present. This has been a problem throughout church history. As early as the second century A.D., believers have speculated about the time and place of the Lord's return.

Unfortunately, unguarded speculation has often prevailed as the most popular approach to biblical prophecy. Some of the wildest possible scenarios have received the most incredible popular support. In a few cases, prophecy has even been used by people as a tool with which they endeavor to justify themselves and condemn their critics.

## Prophetic Interpretation

Every imaginable speculation has arisen as to the identity of the Antichrist, the date of the rapture, and the beginning of the Battle of Armageddon. In our effort to make sense of all this, let us suggest a simple paradigm:

*Facts.* There are the clearly stated facts of prophetic revelation: Christ will return for His own, He will judge the world, there will be a time of great trouble on the earth at the end of the age, the final conflict will be won by Christ, and so on. These basic facts are clearly stated in Scripture.

*Assumptions.* Factual prophecy only tells us so much and no more. Beyond that we must make certain assumptions. If these are correct, they will lead to valid conclusions, but if not, they may lead to baseless speculations. For example, it is an assumption that Russia will invade Israel in the last days. Whether or not that is factual depends on the legitimacy of one's interpretation of Ezekiel's Magog prophecy (Ezekiel 38–39). It is foolish to say we don't need to worry about Russia because it will be destroyed. That is only an assumption based upon one's interpretation of Magog's identity.

*Speculations.* These are purely calculated guesses based on assumptions. In many cases they have no basis in prophetic fact at all. For example, the Bible says the number of the Antichrist is "666" (Revelation 13:18). We can only speculate what this means. It is an assumption that it is a literal number that will appear on things in the last days. When one prominent evangelist saw the number 666 prefixed on automobile license plates in Israel a few years ago, he speculated that the "mark of the Beast" had already arrived in the Holy Land.

## A Variety of Views

One of the challenges of understanding Bible prophecy is that people approach it with different methods of interpretation. Within the Christian church there have been a variety of approaches to the study of eschatology, or the last days. Some even refuse to consider prophecy at all, preferring to dismiss it as hopelessly confusing or generally irrelevant. But among evangelical Christians, prophecy has always been taken seriously.

The issue at stake among evangelicals has generally been *how* a person interprets prophecy. Three main schools of thought have been proposed. While most evangelical Christians are premillennial in their view of eschatology, some are also amillennial or postmillennial.

*Postmillennial.* This school of thought believes that the Millennium (the 1000-year reign of Christ mentioned in Revelation 20:1-3,6-7) is to be interpreted symbolically as synonymous with the church age. Satan's power is viewed as being "bound" by the power of the gospel. Postmillennialists believe that during this Millennium (church age) the church is called upon to conquer unbelief, convert the masses, and govern society by the mandate of biblical law. Only after Christianity succeeds on earth will Christ return and announce that His kingdom has been realized. Advocates of postmillennialism urge believers to take dominion over the earth and its political governments in order to usher in the kingdom of God on earth.

*Amillennial.* This approach sees no Millennium of any kind on the earth. Rather, amillennialists tend to view so-called millennial prophecies as being fulfilled in eternity. Biblical references to the "thousand years" are interpreted symbolically. In this scheme, the church age ends with the return of Christ to judge the world and usher in eternity. God's promises to Israel are viewed as having been fulfilled in the church (the New Israel of the new covenant); therefore, amillennialists see no specific future for national Israel. They view the church age as an era of conflict between the forces of good and evil, which culminates with the return of Christ.

*Premillennial.* This view says that Christ will return at the end of the church age to set up His kingdom on earth for a literal 1000 years. Most premillennialists also believe there will be a period of great tribulation on earth prior to the return of Christ. Some premillennialists believe the church will go through the Tribulation (posttribulationists), others believe the church will be raptured prior to the Tribulation (pretribulationists), and a small number believe the church will be raptured in the middle of the Tribulation (midtribulationists). Despite these differences in regard to the rapture of the church, premillennialists generally believe in the future restoration of the state of Israel and the eventual conversions of the Jews to Christianity.

Most evangelical Christians hold to the dispensational premillennial view of eschatology, which looks forward to the rapture of believers to heaven as the next major prophetic event to be fulfilled. This, they believe, will end the church age and prepare the way for the Tribulation and the return of Christ.

One Bible passage that suggests the rapture is 1 Thessalonians 4:16-17:

> The Lord Himself will descend from heaven with a shout, with the voice of an archangel, and with the trumpet call of God, and the dead in Christ will rise first. Then we who are alive and remain shall be caught up together with them in the clouds to meet the Lord in the air. And thus we shall always be with the Lord.

## Taking Prophecy Seriously

Evangelical Christians take seriously the Bible's prophecies about the end times, the Great Tribulation, Armageddon, and the return of Christ. In fact, many are convinced that the march to Armageddon, the last great battle, has already begun. They sense that the stage is being set and believe we are living in the end times, when the world will be plunged into a series of cataclysmic wars that may well claim three-fourths of the world's population.

In recent years, more and more of the secular community has come to agree that we seem to be approaching the end of the world. Nobel laureates and reputable scientists have warned that the earth's time clock is running out. Air and water pollution, the evaporation of the protective ozone layer, the elimination of oxygen-producing rain forests, and the general instability of the earth's crust have all been cited as serious problems that could hinder the future of life on this planet. The current proliferation of weapons of mass destruction is almost beyond belief, and many of those weapons are suspected to be in the hands of unscrupulous terrorists.

In past centuries, when Christians talked about the end of the world, people often laughed at them because they could not conceive of the entire planet as being destroyed. But today, both Christians and agnostics realize that such destruction is well within the realm of possibility.

The Bible warns us that the "day of the Lord so comes as a thief in the night" (1 Thessalonians 5:1-2). It will be an instantaneous event that will catch the world unprepared. In fact, the Bible reminds us that people will promise, "Peace, peace! when there is no peace" (Jeremiah 8:11; see also Ezekiel 13:10).

Mankind has demonstrated irrevocably that it cannot bring a permanent and lasting peace to this world. Every human effort at peace has been short-lived and destined to failure. At the end of time, when the stakes are the highest, the greatest gamble ever made for peace will end in the greatest battle of all time—at Armageddon.

## Interpreting the Bible Literally

One of the most important factors in studying Bible prophecy is to interpret the text literally. One of the basic rules of biblical interpretation is this: "If the literal sense makes good sense, seek no other sense, lest it result in nonsense." When evangelical Christians read the Bible, we take literally its statements about Jesus' birth in Bethlehem, His ministry in Galilee, the fact that He healed the sick and raised the dead. We believe He was literally crucified, literally buried, and that He literally rose from the dead. So why shouldn't we believe He will literally come back one day?

We understand, of course, that there are times the Bible uses figurative language. For example, Jesus is called the Lamb of God 28 times in the book of Revelation. This does not mean that He is a literal lamb.

The term *lamb,* in reference to Christ, is intended to give us a symbolic picture of Christ as our atoning sacrifice. But the symbolic use of *lamb* does not eliminate the literal truth of Christ as our atoning sacrifice.

The prophecies of Christ's first coming were fulfilled literally in minute detail. Therefore, we have every confidence that the prophecies of His second coming will be fulfilled literally as well. Jesus really is coming back to rapture believers and take them to the Father's house (John 14:1-3). He is also coming again to judge the world, defeat the Antichrist, bind Satan, and bring the kingdom of heaven to earth. That leaves us with only one question: When?

## Lesson 2

# Understanding Bible Prophecy

Too often, Christians have been reluctant to study Bible prophecy because they fear it's too complicated or controversial. But if God included literally hundreds of prophecies in the Bible, surely He did so for a reason! He wants us to know what the future holds. He *wants* us to recognize that He is fully in control, that Christ will rule the world someday, and that we have a wonderful eternity to look forward to. The more you as a Christian understand Bible prophecy, the more you will enjoy the confidence and security that comes from knowing that nothing will change the final outcome that has already been determined by God.

1. The Old Testament contains many prophecies that predict the first coming of Christ and the gift of salvation He would offer. According to 1 Peter 1:10, what attitude did the Old Testament prophets have toward these prophecies? *They wanted to know more*

2. Read 1 Peter 1:12. Who were the Old Testament prophets ministering to when they proclaimed their prophecies? *Us.*

3. And what did the "angels desire to look into"? *watching these thing happen*

4. Virtually the entire book of Revelation is prophetic in nature. What benefit does Revelation 1:3 say will be experienced by "those who hear the words of this prophecy"? *God blesss*

5. We can see, then, that a right attitude toward prophecy is important. In addition, what does Titus 2:12 say about how we should live "in the present age"? *turn from Godles living & sinful pleasures. live with wisdom righteousness & devotion to god*

6. What are we to look for, according to Titus 2:13? *look forward to the return of Christ*

## *Applying Prophecy to Everyday Life*

How is God helping you to better appreciate the importance of
Bible prophecy and what it means to your daily life?

# 3

# ARE WE LIVING IN THE LAST DAYS?

The apostle Paul looked down the corridor of time into the distant future and predicted that "in the last days perilous times will come" (2 Timothy 3:1 NIV). Are those days here now? Is the coming of Christ on the horizon?

The world is changing every day. We are standing on the edge of a new day in world politics. The dramatic changes we have witnessed in Europe, the Middle East, and the former Soviet Union tell us that the world is undergoing a massive transformation. The aftermath of World War II has long since been shaken from us like dust from an old rag. Eastern Europe is awakening to a new day of hope and freedom. But turmoil in the Middle East reminds us the world is still facing difficult days ahead.

At the same time, there is great concern about where all these changes are taking us. Charles Colson recently said, "We sense that things are winding down, that somehow freedom, justice, and order are slipping away. Our great civilization may not yet lie in smoldering ruins, but the enemy is within the gates. The times seem to smell of sunset" (*Against the Night* [Ann Arbor, MI: Servant, 1989], p. 55). He goes on to suggest that Western civilization is facing the greatest crisis encountered since the barbarians invaded Rome.

Many believe we have now moved to the final round in the struggle for world dominion. The collapse of communism has removed one of the significant players in what one writer has called the "Great Millennial Endgame." But the end of the Cold War is by no means the end of the struggle for world supremacy.

Our neglect of God's revelation has pushed us to the limits of our own rationalization. We have abandoned rationality for irrationality in the attempt to hold onto belief in something—anything—beyond ourselves. All through the twentieth century, we allowed godless secularism to replace the Judeo-Christian values of our society. God has been deliberately and systematically removed from prominence in our culture and in our intellectual lives. We have made Him irrelevant to our culture.

Tragically, we have also made our culture irrelevant to God. In so doing, we have abandoned our spiritual heritage. The Christian consensus that once dominated Western culture is now shattered. The world is already mired in the quicksand of secularism, relativism, and mysticism. In the place of biblical Christianity, people are now calling for the New World Order, which consists of the very elements Scripture warns will signify the empire of the Antichrist:

1. World Government—Globalists are now insisting that national governments should surrender their sovereignty to a one-world government. Such a government would operate through a world headquarters, a world court, and even a world military. Today, there are many serious voices calling for such a reality.

2. World Economy—The rampant spread of globalism is fueled by the driving force of the world economy. It is virtually impossible to do business today without networking with the global economy. There is almost no such thing as an "American" product that is not dependent on parts, trade, or investments from foreign countries.

3. World Religion—This will be the final phase of the New World Order. The idea of a new world religion or peace and cooperation is already being proposed. Religious unity has been endorsed by Catholic popes, the Dalai Lama, and leaders of the World Council of Churches.

What we are witnessing today may well be the fulfillment of the biblical prophecies of the end times. Revelation 13 predicts the rise of a powerful world ruler who is able to control the world politically and economically. This ruler will have at his side a false prophet who promotes a one-world religion.

## The New World Order

Today there is a new wave of optimism sweeping across Europe. The economic unification of the European Union is now well under way. The Europe of the future may well become a political union, the United States of Europe. If this happens, Europe, not America, will be the strongest and most powerful "nation" on earth—economically, politically, and even militarily. And if the current European Union were to continue to expand into the former Soviet satellites of Eastern Europe and even into Russia itself, Europe would stretch from the Atlantic Ocean to the Pacific Ocean for the first time in history!

The key players in the New Europe will be England, France, Germany, and Russia. The unification or cooperation of these four superstates could well determine the issue of who controls the world of the future.

Many Christians believe that the resurgence of the New Europe fulfills the biblical prophecies of a revived Roman Empire in the last days. Like the architects of the Tower of Babel, advocates of the New World Order believe that "coming together" will consolidate what were formerly volatile or weak economies and foster global peace and cooperation. Helmut Kohl has said, "The United States of Europe will form the core of a peaceful order...the age prophesied of old, when all shall dwell secure and none shall make them afraid" (*The European,* October 11, 1991, p. 1).

The real tragedy in all this talk of global unity is the absence of any emphasis on the spiritual roots of democracy and freedom. The gospel has been blunted in Western Europe for so long that there is little God-consciousness left in the European people. Without Christ, the Prince of Peace, there can be no hope for man-made orders of peace and prosperity. There will be no Millennium without the Messiah!

## Where Are We Now?

What is now more clear than ever is that we have taken a quantum leap toward the fulfillment of the biblical prophecies of the last days. The stage is now being set for the final climactic act in the long history of the human drama. The stage for the fulfillment of the prophecies of the end times is now set:

1. The fall of communism has paved the way for a world economy and a world government. The global web is tightening around us every day.

2. Secularism is giving way to New Age mysticism as the do-it-yourself religion of our times. The end result will be the watering down of religious beliefs so that they are more palatable to the general public.

3. Global economic interdependence will eventually lead to global political system that dominates national sovereignty.

4. Materialism and selfism will replace spiritual values. Mankind will be left in the mindless pursuit of material prosperity as the basis for meaning and value in life.

5. The spiritual vacuum that results will leave the world ready for the ultimate deception: The Great Lie of the Antichrist that will deceive the whole world.

6. A world leader will quickly arise on the international scene promising to bring peace and economic stability. He will receive the support of the European community and eventually control the whole world.

7. A crisis in the Middle East will trigger this world leader's intervention militarily and politically. He will eventually sign a peace treaty with Israel, only to break it later.

8. A false prophet of international fame will suddenly emerge to gain control of the world religious system and use it to reinforce the worship of Antichrist.

9. All resistance to the world system will be crushed by a massive worldwide persecution. Men, women, and children will be slaughtered in the name of the World State.

10. Israel will become the central figure in the conflict with the World State. The Antichrist will eventually break his covenant with Israel and invade her land, setting the stage for the Battle of Armageddon.

## How Close Are We to the End?

There is no doubt in our minds that we are fast approaching the final chapter of human history. The hoof beats of the four horsemen of the Apocalypse can now be heard in the distance. The stage is set for the final act of human drama. The clock is ticking away the last seconds of any hope for a reprieve. We are being swept down the corridor of time to an inevitable date with destiny.

How much time is left? Only God knows. We must use every means at our disposal to preach the gospel of God's saving grace everywhere we can while there is still time. This is not the time to rest on our laurels. Rather, we have a window of opportunity, by the grace of God, and we need to take advantage of it right now. It is time for us Western Christians to take seriously our responsibility to evangelize the world in our lifetime.

If we do not meet this challenge and fulfill our obligation, every kind of false religious cult, every kind of cast secular materialism, and every kind of moral perversion will rush to fill that vacuum. We alone have the truth that can set the world free from spiritual oppression. We must be willing to do all we can to fill that void—now!

Jesus Christ said what we all must realize at this crucial hour: "As long as it is day, we must do the work of him who sent me. Night is coming, when no one can work" (John 9:4 NIV). To the ancient church at Philadelphia, our Lord said, "I have set before you an open door, and no one can shut it" (Revelation 3:8). God has also given today's church an open door to preach the gospel where it has not yet been heard. May we rise to the occasion, recognizing that the ultimate struggle for world dominion is between the forces of Christ and the forces of evil.

## Lesson 3

# Are We Living in the Last Days?

We twenty-first century Christians live in exciting times. While we don't know exactly when Christ will return, we do know that His coming is drawing closer and closer. The evidence around us indicates more and more that we live in the very kind of society the Bible warned would arise in the days before the second coming. It's fascinating to watch as history continues to unfold, and as we see the Scripture's description of the last days become reality before our very eyes.

1. Read John 14:1-3. What does verse 2 say Jesus is doing right now? What promise does Jesus give in verse 3? *preparing a place* *Jesus is coming to get us.*

2. When Jesus talked about the destruction of the Temple in Matthew 24:1-2, what two questions did the disciples ask in response (see verse 3)? *when will do take place i will there be a sign*

3. What was Jesus' ultimate answer to the disciples (see verse 36)? *even Jesus doesn't know — only the Father knows*

4. Because it's impossible for us to predict when Jesus will return, some Christians decide it's not important for us to "study the times." But what exhortation are we given in Ephesians 5:15-16? Why? *walk wisely because the days are evil*

5. What will people be like in the last days, according to 2 Timothy 3:1-5? How many of these characteristics do you see manifest in our world today? *bad they may be religious but will not know God — all these characteristics*

6. What additional problems will arise in the last days, according to 2 Timothy 4:2-4? *people won't want to know the truth*

7. How are we to respond to these problems (see 2 Timothy 4:2,5)? *persistently preaching.*

## *Applying Prophecy to Everyday Life*

Read 2 Timothy 2:15. Do you consider yourself well-enough versed in the Bible to help do your part in defending against wrong teaching and wrong living? What improvements would you like to make? *need to know more,*

4

# The Rapture of the Church

One of the most compelling and exciting prophetic events described in the Bible is the rapture of the Church. It is clearly taught in 1 Thessalonians chapter 4, where the apostle Paul provides us with these details:

> This we say to you by the word of the Lord, that we who are alive and remain until the coming of the Lord will by no means precede those who are asleep. For the Lord Himself will descend from heaven with a shout, with the voice of an archangel, and with the trumpet of God. And the dead in Christ will rise first. Then we who are alive and remain shall be caught up together with them in the clouds to meet the Lord in the air. And thus we shall always be with the Lord. Therefore comfort one another with these words (verses 15-18).

From this passage of Scripture, we can see that there are five stages to the rapture:

1. The Lord Himself will descend from heaven with a shout and with the sound of a trumpet.

2. The dead in Christ will rise first.

3. Then we who are alive and remain on the earth will be caught up together with them in the clouds.

4. We will meet the Lord in the air.

5. And we will always be with Him.

The English word *rapture* comes from the Latin *rapto*, which is a translation of the Greek word *harpazo* in the Greek New Testament. All these terms mean "caught up" or "snatched away." While the word *rapture* does not appear in English translations, the concept of the rapture certainly does.

## The Mystery of the Rapture

The apostle Paul also unveiled what he referred to as a mystery pertaining to the rapture. He explained that there would be some Christians who would not sleep (die), but whose bodies would be instantly transformed:

> Behold, I tell you a mystery: We shall not all sleep, but we shall all be changed—in a moment, in the twinkling of an eye, at the last trumpet. For the trumpet will sound, and the dead will be raised incorruptible, and we shall be changed. For this corruptible must put on incorruption, and this mortal must put on immortality (1 Corinthians 15:51-53).

Without warning, at the moment of the rapture, the bodies of all believers who have died since the day of Pentecost will suddenly be transformed into new, living, immortal, resurrected bodies. Even those whose bodies have long since decayed or whose ashes have been scattered across the oceans will receive a new body. This new body will be joined together with the person's spirit, which Jesus brings with Him from heaven. Then the bodies of those who are alive on earth and have accepted Christ as their Savior will also be instantly translated into new, immortal bodies.

What's more, note the similarity of the descriptions of the rapture in 1 Corinthians 15:51-53 and 2 Thessalonians 4:15-18. When Christ comes to take His church (all believers) to heaven in fulfillment of His promise in John 14:1-3, He will include all New Testament believers, both the living and the dead.

Together, all believers will be instantaneously transported into the heavens to meet first their loved ones "in the clouds" and then to meet the Lord in the air. Those who have rejected the salvation of Jesus Christ and remain on earth will witness a miraculous event of astonishing proportions—the sudden mass disappearance of millions upon millions of Christians from the face of the earth.

The rapture is often referred to as "the blessed hope" (Titus 2:13) because it provides comfort not only to those believers who are concerned about the coming Tribulation, but also to those who long to be reunited with their departed loved ones who share faith in Christ.

The second coming, which encompasses both the rapture and the glorious appearing, is one of the most significant events mentioned in the entire Bible. There are 321 references in the New Testament alone of this awesome event, making it the second most prominent doctrine presented in Scripture after salvation.

The doctrine of the second coming is clearly taught in both the Old and New Testaments. It is also affirmed in the doctrinal statement of every major Christian denomination. On average, the New Testament mentions the second coming in one out of every 30 verses, and it is mentioned in every chapter of 1 and 2 Thessalonians, the first books written for the early church. Moreover, all nine New Testament authors mention the second coming, and 23 of the 27 New Testament books reference it. Obviously God intended His church to be motivated to holiness, evangelism, and missionary concern by the study of the second coming of Christ.

## Two Phases of the Second Coming

When the biblical references pertaining to the second coming are carefully examined, it becomes clear that there are two distinct phases to Christ's return. There are simply too many conflicting elements in these phases to merge them into a single event. In the first phase, Jesus will come suddenly to rapture His church in the air and take all believers to His Father's house in fulfillment of His promise in John 14:1-3. There, they will appear before the judgment seat of Christ (2 Corinthians 5:9-10) and participate in the marriage supper of the Lamb (Revelation 19:1-10).

During this time, those left behind on the earth will experience the trials of the horrendous seven-year Tribulation period. Then Jesus will conclude the Tribulation with the second phase of His second coming by returning to Earth in great power and glory to stop the slaughter and set up His millennial kingdom. So the entire second coming could be compared to a two-act play (the rapture and the glorious appearance) separated by a seven-year intermission (the Tribulation). The apostle Paul distinguishes between these two phases in Titus 2:13, where he refers to the rapture as "the blessed hope" and the return of Christ to the earth as the "glorious appearing."

There are some theologians who attempt to dismiss the multiphase aspect of Christ's second coming. They place both the rapture and the glorious appearing at the end of the Tribulation, and hold to what is known as the posttribulation view of the rapture. In this scenario, Christians will be required to face the horrors of the Tribulation.

In order to hold this view, one must either spiritualize away or simply ignore numerous passages of Scripture. A careful study of the many biblical references to the second coming clearly shows that the rapture and the glorious appearing are two separate phases of the second coming. Consider the following differences:

| The Rapture of the Church | The Glorious Appearing |
|---|---|
| 1. Christ comes *for* believers in the air. | 1. Christ comes *with* believers to the Earth. |

| The Rapture of the Church | The Glorious Appearing |
|---|---|
| 2. All Christians on Earth are translated into new bodies. | 2. There is no translation of bodies. |
| 3. Christians are taken to the Father's house in heaven. | 3. Resurrected saints remain on the Earth. |
| 4. There is no judgment upon the Earth. | 4. Christ judges the inhabitants of the Earth. |
| 5. The church will be taken to heaven. | 5. Christ sets up His kingdom on Earth. |
| 6. It could occur at any time (it is imminent). | 6. It cannot occur until the end of the seven-year Tribulation period. |
| 7. There are no signs preceding it. | 7. There are numerous signs preceding it. |
| 8. It affects only believers. | 8. It affects all humanity. |
| 9. It is a time of joy. | 9. It is a time of mourning. |
| 10. It occurs before the "day of wrath." | 10. It occurs after the "day of wrath." |
| 11. Satan is not bound, but wreaks havoc on the Earth. | 11. Satan is bound in the abyss for 1000 years. |
| 12. Christians are judged at the judgment seat of Christ. | 12. Christians have already been judged at the judgment seat. |

| The Rapture of the Church | The Glorious Appearing |
|---|---|
| 13. The Marriage of the Lamb takes place. | 13. The Marriage of the Lamb has already taken place. |
| 14. Only Christ's own will see Him. | 14. All those on Earth will see Him. |
| 15. The seven-year Tribulation follows. | 15. The 1000-year Millennium follows. |

While various views exist as to *when* the rapture will occur (before, during, or after the Tribulation), all must acknowledge that there will be a rapture. The only real question is, *When* will it occur? Christ must return at some point to resurrect the "dead in Christ" and rapture the living believers in order to take us all to the Father's house in heaven, as Jesus promised in John 14:1-4. There are a number of reasons to believe the rapture will occur *before* the Tribulation begins, including these promises of a pretribulational rapture:

1. *The Lord Himself promised to deliver us.* Revelation 3:10 says, "Because you have kept My command to persevere, I also will keep you from the hour of trial which shall come upon the whole world, to test those who dwell on the earth." The Greek word *ek*, which literally means "out of," is translated in this passage as "from." In other words, it is the Lord's intention to keep the church *out of* the Tribulation. Therefore, the rapture must occur before the Tribulation begins.

2. *The church is to be delivered from the wrath to come.* The apostle Paul tells us in 1 Thessalonians 1:10 that we should "wait for His Son from heaven, whom He raised from the dead, even Jesus who delivers us from the wrath to come." The context of this particular passage is the rapture. The church must

therefore be removed from the earth before the Tribulation begins in order to be delivered from the wrath to come.

3. *The church is not appointed to wrath.* According to 1 Thessalonians 5:9, "God did not appoint us to wrath, but to obtain salvation through our Lord Jesus Christ." Likewise, as Jesus Himself promises in Revelation 3:10, "I also will keep you from the hour of trial which shall come upon the whole world, to test those who dwell on the earth." Once again, the context of these passages is the rapture. Since the Tribulation is prophesied as a time of God's wrath, and since Christians are not appointed to wrath, it follows that the church must be raptured out of the way before the Tribulation begins.

4. *The church is absent in Revelation chapters 4–18.* Revelation chapters 4–18 detail the events of the Tribulation. The church is mentioned 17 times in the first three chapters of Revelation, but after John (who is a member of the church) is taken up to heaven at the beginning of chapter 4, the church is not mentioned or seen again until chapter 19 when she appears at the marriage with Christ in heaven and then returns to earth with Jesus at His glorious appearing. Why is she missing from those chapters? Because the church isn't in the Tribulation. She will be raptured out before it begins.

5. *If the church is raptured at the end of the Tribulation, there will be no one left to re-populate the Earth during the Millennium.* Just before the Millennium begins, all sinners (those who reject Jesus Christ as Savior) who have survived the Tribulation will be cast into hell, according to Matthew 25:46. Should the rapture occur at the end of the Tribulation, as some believe, all Christians would be taken from the earth as well, leaving no one on earth with a natural body to re-populate the planet during the Millennium. The problem here is that we know from numerous Old Testament passages, as well as Revelation 20:7-10, that there will be a huge population explosion during the Millennium. Where do these people come from? The answer is that those who miss the rapture

and become believers during the Tribulation (thanks to the preaching of the 144,000 Jews and the two witnesses) and survive to the end will re-populate the earth. While large numbers of believers will be martyred during the Tribulation, there will be some who survive. These people will not be raptured at the end of the Tribulation in some sort of post-tribulational rapture, but rather, will enter Christ's millennial kingdom with their natural bodies to populate that kingdom. In order for this to be possible, the rapture must take place prior to the Tribulation instead of at the end of it.

Among the chief characteristics of the rapture is that it will be sudden and will catch people by surprise. "Of that day and hour no one knows" (Matthew 24:36), which is why we should live so as to "be ready, for the Son of Man is coming at an hour when you do not expect" (Matthew 24:44). Only a pretribulation rapture preserves the at-any-moment expectation of His coming. Indeed, throughout the ages, the rapture has appeared imminent to Christians of every generation. Nothing could better motivate us to holy living and fervent evangelism than to believe that Jesus could come today. And one day He will! The trumpet will sound, the archangel will shout, and we will all go home to be with Jesus.

# EVENTS OF THE RAPTURE

1. The Lord Himself will descend from His Father's house, where He is preparing a place for us (John 14:1-3; 1 Thessalonians 4:16).

2. He will come again to receive us to Himself (John 14:1-3).

3. He will resurrect those who have fallen asleep in Him (deceased believers whom we will not precede—1 Thessalonians 4:14-15).

4. The Lord will shout as He descends ("loud command," 1 Thessalonians 4:16 NIV). All this takes place in the "twinkling of an eye" (1 Corinthians 15:52).

5. We will hear the voice of the archangel (perhaps to lead Israel during the seven years of the Tribulation as he did in the Old Testament—1 Thessalonians 4:16).

6. We will also hear the trumpet call of God (1 Thessalonians 4:16), the last trumpet for the church. (Don't confuse this with the seventh trumpet of judgment upon the world during the Tribulation in Revelation 11:15.)

7. The dead in Christ will rise first (the corruptible ashes of their dead bodies are made incorruptible and joined together with their spirits,

which Jesus brings with Him—1 Thessalonians 4:16-17).

8. Then we who are alive and remain will be changed (or made incorruptible by having our bodies made "immortal"—1 Corinthians 15:51,53).

9. We will be caught up (raptured) together (1 Thessalonians 4:17).

10. We will be caught up in the clouds (where dead—and living believers will have a monumental reunion—1 Thessalonians 4:17).

11. We will meet the Lord in the air (1 Thessalonians 4:17).

12. Christ will receive us to Himself and take us to the Father's house "that where I am, there you may be also" (John 14:3).

13. "And so we shall always be with the Lord" (1 Thessalonians 4:17).

14. At the call of Christ for believers, He will judge all things. Christians will stand before the judgment seat of Christ (Romans 14:10; 2 Corinthians 5:10), described in detail in 1 Corinthians 3:11-15. This judgment prepares Christians for...

15. The marriage of the Lamb. Before Christ returns to earth in power and great glory, He will meet His bride, the church, and the marriage supper will take place. In the meantime, after the church is raptured, the world will suffer the unprecedented outpouring of God's wrath, which our Lord called "the great tribulation" (Matthew 24:21).

The Father's House

Judgment Seat
1 Corinthians 3:9-15

John 14:1-3

Rapture
1 Thessalonians 4:16-17
1 Corinthians 15:51-58

Church Age

Tribulation 7 Years

Millennium 1000 Years

Excerpted from Tim LaHaye and Thomas Ice, *Charting the End Times* (Eugene, OR: Harvest House Publishers, 2001), p. 51.

## Lesson 4

# The Rapture of the Church

A careful look at the Bible shows that there are no more prophecies that must be fulfilled in order for the rapture to occur. In
other words, the rapture—the moment in which Christ will take
all New Testament believers up to heaven prior to the seven-year
Tribulation—is the very next event that will take place on God's
prophetic calendar. We know it *will* happen; we just don't know
*when*.

1. Write here the five stages of the rapture, as described
   in 1 Thessalonians 4:15-18 and in the list
   on pages 31-32:
   - —
   - —
   - —
   - —
   - —

2. List here the five reasons for believing in a pretribulation rapture, and write down the supporting verse
   reference, as given on pages 34-36.
   - —
   - —
   - —
   - —
   - —

3. What specific action does Jesus say we're to take in
   regard to the rapture, according to Mark 13:32-33?

4. Read 1 John 2:28. What are we told to do in order to be
   ready for the coming of Christ?

———◦———

## *Applying Prophecy to Everyday Life*

Why is it so important for us to live as though Christ could come
at any moment? Try to come up with at least two or three reasons.

# 5

# THE BELIEVER'S REWARDS

For the Bible-believing Christian, the second coming of Christ is one of the most eagerly anticipated events prophesied in the Bible. It's hard not to get excited when we read that

> the Lord Himself will descend from heaven with a shout, with the voice of an archangel, and with the trumpet of God. And the dead in Christ will rise first. Then we who are alive and remain shall be caught up together with them in the clouds to meet the Lord in the air. And thus we shall always be with the Lord (1 Thessalonians 4:16-17).

We all have friends and loved ones who have passed on and whom we long to be reunited with. As ecstatic as that experience would be, it will be eclipsed by our first meeting with the very Lord who died for us, forgave us, saved us, guided us through life, and resurrected us. Words will not be able to adequately express the joy of that moment.

What tends to get overlooked in all this is that immediately following the rapture, we will stand before the judgment seat of Christ and give an account of our actions while on earth.

## Christ Will Be Our Judge

First Corinthians 4:5 tells us to "judge nothing before the time, until the Lord comes, who will both bring to light the hidden things of darkness and reveal the counsels of the hearts." This clearly says that the Lord will judge us at His coming. Many Christians have been lulled into a false state of complacency regarding this judgment. Some think there is no call on their life to serve the Lord. Consequently, they accept His salvation as a gift and do nothing to advance His kingdom. If Christians truly understood the eternal significance of good works, they would radically alter their lifestyle.

> By grace you have been saved through faith, and that not of yourselves; it is the gift of God, not of works, lest anyone should boast. For we are His workmanship, created in Christ Jesus for good works, which God prepared beforehand that we should walk in them (Ephesians 2:8-10).

Although we are indeed saved by grace and not by our works, the Lord still expects us, once saved, to do good works for Him. In fact, we will be rewarded in the life to come in direct proportion to the way in which we have served Him. "We must all appear before the judgment seat of Christ, that each one may receive the things done in the body, according to what he has done, whether good or bad" (2 Corinthians 5:10).

### *Judgment Seat of Christ*

This judgment of our works will determine our position of service during the Millennium and may affect our status in heaven throughout eternity. This judgment of believers, which takes place at the judgment seat (Greek, *bema*) of Christ in heaven following the rapture, is a time of reward and is not to be confused with the Great White Throne judgment of unbelievers (Revelation 20:11-15). The *bema* seat judgment of believers is detailed in the following passage of Scripture:

> No other foundation can anyone lay than that which is laid, which is Jesus Christ. Now if anyone builds on this foundation with gold, silver, precious stones, wood, hay, straw, each

one's work will become clear; for the Day will declare it, because it will be revealed by fire; and the fire will test each one's work, of what sort it is. If anyone's work which he has built on it endures, he will receive a reward. If anyone's work is burned, he will suffer loss; but he himself will be saved, yet so as through fire (1 Corinthians 3:11-15).

While the unsaved world is experiencing the horrendous seven-year Tribulation period on Earth, believers will be standing before their Lord in judgment to receive rewards based on their good works. It should be noted that only believers will experience this judgment, and at no time will their eternal salvation be in jeopardy. Our eternal destiny is secure. In contrast, all unbelievers will stand before the Great White Throne Judgment at the end of the Millennium, during which their eternal destiny will be determined by their works. Because their works cannot save them, all of them will be cast into the lake of fire.

## Significance of Good Works

What exactly is a good work? A good work is anything a Christian does for Jesus Christ. Examples would include witnessing, worshiping, and generosity toward others, along with an infinite number of other activities. Jesus made it clear that nothing is too small to be considered a good work. Matthew 10:42 reveals that even giving a cup of cold water to a child would result in divine compensation. Good works performed with impure motives, however, will not be rewarded.

When it comes to good works, as 1 Corinthians 3:11-15 indicates, the foundation of Jesus Christ must first be in place. This means that no one can accumulate good works until he has accepted salvation through Christ. Once that occurs, a person can build upon that foundation with works represented by "gold, silver, precious stones, wood, hay, straw." These works will be tested by fire. The metals and precious stones represent good works performed with right motives. They will survive the test of fire and be rewarded. The wood, hay, and straw represent bad works and will not survive the test. These would include good works performed with either bad motives, a hidden agenda, or unconfessed sin in one's life.

There are a number of stories in the Bible that illustrate the varying level of rewards that will be handed out. The parable of Luke 19:11-27 explains that Jesus expects a certain quantity of works relative to what has been entrusted to us. It tells of a nobleman who gave an equal amount of money to his servants to invest while he was away. When he returned, he found that one servant had increased the nobleman's original investment by ten times. The nobleman was very pleased and made the servant ruler over ten cities. Another servant increased the nobleman's money by five times and was given charge over five cities. This illustration demonstrates that our rewards will be proportionate to the degree we have used our God-given opportunities to serve Him. All Christians should understand that God expects results from our lives.

Another parable, found in Matthew 25:14-30, tells of a master who gave five talents to one servant and two to another. The servant with five talents earned five more, while the one with two earned two more. In this case, both servants received the same reward because they both made good use of what had been given to them. Likewise, God will hold us accountable for using what talents, abilities, and opportunities He has given us for His service. Fortunately, we have a just God who will treat each believer according to his or her natural abilities. More will be expected from those of higher privilege, as demonstrated by the verse that reads, "To whom much is given, from him much will be required" (Luke 12:48).

Now, this doesn't mean that the thought of heavenly rewards should be our motivation for serving Christ. Rather, our motivation should be out of love. But at the same time, we should recognize and act upon Jesus' challenge that we invest wisely in eternity.

> Do not lay up for yourselves treasures on earth, where moth and rust destroy and where thieves break in and steal; but lay up for yourselves treasures in heaven, where neither moth nor rust destroys and where thieves do not break in and steal. For where your treasure is, there your heart will be also (Matthew 6:19-21).

# JUDGMENT OF BELIEVERS AT THE JUDGMENT SEAT OF CHRIST
## 1 Corinthians 3:11-15

**Good Works**
Ephesians 2:10

1. **Quality**
   Matthew 25:14-30

2. **Quantity**
   Luke 19:11-27

3. **Time**
   Matthew 20:1-16

**Warning**
2 John 8

**Bad Works**

1. **Good works done with evil motives**
   Matthew 6:2

2. **Hidden counsels**
   I Corinthians 4:5

3. **Unconfessed sin**
   I John 1:9

## The Believer's Crowns

Scripture promises crowns to those whose works survive the test of fire at the judgment seat of Christ. Crowns are for rulers, and according to Revelation 20:6, we will rule and reign with Christ in His millennial kingdom. In certain parables, Jesus told of faithful servants who were subsequently appointed to rule over cities. That may be the reason the judgment seat of Christ takes place just prior to the start of His millennial kingdom. Apparently Christians will be assigned to specific areas of service in the kingdom directly proportionate to the amount of good works performed while alive on Earth.

According to the Scriptures, there are at least five types of crowns:

1. *The Crown of Righteousness* is for those who live a righteous life—a difficult task in this unrighteous age.
2. *The Crown of Victory* is for those who deny themselves the good things in life in order to better serve their Lord.
3. *The Crown of Life* is for those who are persecuted and martyred while serving the Lord.
4. *The Crown of Rejoicing* is for those who focus their service on winning souls for Christ.
5. *The Crown of Glory* is for those who teach the Word of God faithfully to others.

While the judgment seat of Christ will be an exciting experience for the faithful servant of God, it may be quite sobering for those who during their life on Earth loved the things of the world to the exclusion of serving their Lord. As the Bible indicates, what we do here on Earth will determine how we will serve the Lord during the millennial kingdom. In the final analysis, it is up to each one of us how we will spend those 1000 years.

## Serving in the Kingdom

The millennial kingdom will be a time unlike any other in Earth's history. Christ Himself will establish a kingdom of peace and prosperity on a newly refurbished Earth (2 Peter 3:10); the curse will be lifted from the land; and man's inhumanity to his fellow man will be a thing of the past. There will be two kinds of people on the earth during this period—one natural, and one supernatural. There will be those with natural bodies who survived the seven-year Tribulation (consisting of Jews and those who helped the Jews). And there will be those in resurrected, immortal bodies who have come to the earth from heaven with Christ. Those of us in the resurrected bodies will help Jesus rule and reign over those who still possess natural bodies. And our role in helping Jesus Christ rule over this future kingdom will be determined by our actions of today.

Tragically, two of the greatest enemies of Christian service, selfishness and laziness, have cheated many of God's people out of the rewards they could have received. Second John 8 warns, it is possible to "lose those things we worked for." Although we will not lose our salvation, it's possible to forfeit our rewards by indulging in temptation. The Bible says we reap what we sow (see Galatians 6:7). This life serves as a time of planting, while the next life results in the harvest. Just as the farmer must work hard in the spring in order to harvest a crop in the fall, we must dedicate ourselves to serving Christ now in order to receive our rewards in eternity. This truth should motivate believers toward a better life of Christian service.

> Therefore, my beloved brethren, be steadfast, immovable, always abounding in the work of the Lord, knowing that your labor is not in vain in the Lord (1 Corinthians 15:58).

The Bible makes it clear that God is keeping the records. No one serves the Lord who will not be rewarded for that service. In addressing this very issue, Jesus promised to reward every believer "according to his works" at the time of His second coming (Matthew 16:27). While we should not serve Christ merely to earn rewards, He assures us that we will indeed be rewarded for our faithful service to Him.

# The Believer's Rewards

Romans 8:1 promises that there is "no condemnation to those who are in Christ Jesus." We do not need to fear punishment for our sins, because Christ has paid the price for them. Because of Christ's work on the cross, those who have accepted His gift of salvation will spend eternity in heaven, and not in hell.

While we will *not* be judged for our sins (a judgment Christ already took for us), immediately after the rapture, we *will* face a judgment in which we will be rewarded according to our works on earth. Are you ready for this?

1. Read 1 Corinthians 3:11-15. Who is the foundation upon which we should build (verse 11)?

2. What different building materials are listed in verse 12?

3. What will the fire do, according to verse 13?

4. Who will receive a reward (verse 14)?

5. What warning is given in verse 15?

6. The works that will receive rewards are called "good works." We find many examples of good works all through the Bible, but there are some specific passages well worth paying attention to.

7. What good works do you find mentioned in Romans 12:9-18?

8. What are we to do—and not do—according to Ephesians 4:29-32?

9. What encouragement are we given about "doing good" in Galatians 6:9?

10. What exhortation are we given in Galatians 6:10?

## *Applying Prophecy to Everyday Life*

How should the knowledge that you will one day be rewarded for your works on earth affect the way you live?

# 6

# RISE OF THE ANTICHRIST

The Bible clearly predicts the rise of the Antichrist in the end times. As civilization speeds toward its final destiny, the appearance of a powerful world ruler is inevitable. The key question facing our generation is whether he is already alive and well and moving into power. How can we know who he is? What clues are there to his identity? When will he make his move to control the global economy and world politics?

While the Antichrist is a major end-times figure, the term "antichrist" appears only in 1 John 2:18-22; 4:3 and 2 John 7. The apostle John uses it both in the singular ("the Antichrist") and in the plural ("many Antichrists"). John indicates that his readers have already heard that *the* Antichrist is coming in the future. Then he surprises them by announcing that *many* antichrists have already come. He defines these lesser antichrists as liars who deny that Jesus is the Christ (2:22). In this sense, an antichrist is any false teacher who denies the person and word of Jesus Christ. Such teachers are truly *anti* ("against") Christ.

In 1 John 4:1-3, John warns us to test the spirits to make sure they are from God. Again, he warns that many false prophets have "gone out into the world" (NIV). These are the people who don't acknowledge that Jesus is from God. In this sense, John announces that the "spirit of the Antichrist…is now already in the world."

## Spirit of the Antichrist

In the broadest use of the concept of the "spirit of the Antichrist," we can say with certainty that this anti-Christian spirit is already at work. It does everything it can to undermine, deny, and reject the truth about Jesus Christ. That spirit has been here since the first century, actively opposing the work of Christ on earth.

From the very beginning of the Christian era, believers were convinced that a world ruler would eventually come on the scene who was the embodiment of Satan. The book of Revelation (chapters 12–13) presents an "unholy trinity" that aligns Satan (vs. Father), Antichrist (vs. Son), and False Prophet (vs. Holy Spirit). Thus, the real power behind the Antichrist is Satan. The "father of lies" is the perpetrator of the human manifestation of the world's greatest liar and the source of the lie that will condemn multitudes under divine judgment (2 Thessalonians 2:11).

## Titles of the Antichrist

The person we commonly refer to as the Antichrist is known by several names and titles throughout the Bible. Each one provides a glimpse of the many facets of his diabolical character and nature and presents a portrait that leaves little to the imagination.

*The Beast*—"I saw a beast rising up out of the sea, having seven heads and ten horns, and on his horns ten crowns, and on his heads a blasphemous name" (Revelation 13:1).

*The Man of Destruction*—"Let no one deceive you by any means; for that Day will not come unless the falling away comes first, and the man of sin is revealed, the son of perdition" (2 Thessalonians 2:3).

*The Lawless One*—"The lawless one will be revealed, whom the Lord

Jesus will consume with the breath of his mouth and destroy with the brightness of his coming" (2 Thessalonians 2:8).

*The Abomination*—"When you see the 'abomination of desolation,' spoken of by Daniel the prophet, standing in the holy place" (Matthew 24:15).

*The Little Horn*—"I was considering the horns, and there was another horn, a little one, coming up among them, before whom three of the first horns were plucked out by the roots. And there, in this horn, were eyes like the eyes of a man, and a mouth speaking pompous words" (Daniel 7:8).

*The Insolent King*—"In the latter time of their kingdom, when the transgressors have reached their fullness, a king shall arise, having fierce features" (Daniel 8:23).

*The Ruler Who Is to Come*—"After the sixty-two weeks Messiah shall be cut off...and the people of the prince who is to come shall destroy the city and the sanctuary" (Daniel 9:26).

*The Despicable Person*—"He will be succeeded by a contemptible person who has not been given the honor of royalty. He will invade the kingdom when its people feel secure, and he will seize it through intrigue" (Daniel 11:21 NIV).

*The Strong-Willed King*—"The king shall do according to his own will; he shall exalt and magnify himself above every god, shall speak blasphemies against the God of gods, and shall prosper till the wrath has been accomplished; for what has been determined shall be done" (Daniel 11:36).

*The Worthless Shepherd*—"I will raise up a shepherd in the land who will not care for those who are cut off, nor seek the young, nor heal those that are broken, nor feed those that still stand. But he will eat the flesh of the fat and tear their hooves in pieces. Woe to the worthless shepherd, who leaves the flock!" (Zechariah 11:16-17).

*The Antichrist*—"Little children, it is the last hour; and as you have heard that the Antichrist is coming, even now many antichrists have come....Who is a liar, but he who denies that Jesus is the Christ? He is antichrist who denies the Father and the Son" (1 John 2:18,22).

A great deal has been written about the prefix *anti* in connection with the Antichrist. It can mean either "against" (in opposition to) or "instead of" (in place of). The issue comes down to whether he is the great enemy of Christ or he is a false Christ. If he is the enemy of Christ and the head of a Gentile world government, then he is most likely to be a Gentile himself. If he is a false messiah who is accepted by the Jews, then it would stand to reason that he would be Jewish.

## Nationality of the Antichrist

Whether the Antichrist is a Jew or a Gentile is not clearly answered in the New Testament. Most prophetic scholars believe he will be a Gentile because...

- he leads the European Union of Gentile nations (Daniel 7:8-24)
- he will be the leader of the people who destroyed the Temple (i.e., the Romans)
- his covenant with Israel promises Gentile protection for Israel (Daniel 9:27)
- his rule is part of the "times of the Gentiles" and their domination over Israel (Luke 21:24)*

Both Daniel and Revelation associate the Antichrist with a confederation of ten European nations that correspond in some way to the old Roman Empire. Daniel 2:31-45 symbolizes this by the ten *toes* of the great statue in Nebuchadnezzar's dream. Daniel 7:19-28 and Revelation 13:1-9 symbolize this by the ten *horns* on the beast.

In Daniel's prophecies, the Antichrist is always associated with the final phase of the Roman Empire (fourth kingdom). In Revelation 17:9, he is identified with a city that sits on "seven hills" (Rome). While John uses the symbolic term "Mystery Babylon" to describe this city, the mention of seven hills clearly indicates that he is talking about Rome.

---

* These passages make it clear the Antichrist will lead the Western powers. While they do not specifically designate him as a Gentile, they certainly imply that he is a Gentile. The fact that the verse that says he will not regard the "God of his fathers" (KJV) can also be translated "gods of his fathers" (NIV). This makes his background inconclusive. Also, the typical exegesis of Daniel 11:37 has focused on his atheistic beliefs, regardless of whether he is a Jew or Gentile.

It is not difficult, given our current international interconnectedness and the need for a human leader who can guarantee a peaceful coexistence among the nations, to imagine a powerful world ruler coming on the scene in the immediate future. The same spirit of Antichrist is at work today, attempting to lure this world into the lap of Satan.

## Genius and Power of the Antichrist

The Antichrist will be one of the most astounding leaders the world has ever known. On the surface he will appear to be the epitome of human genius and power, for he will possess…

- intellectual genius (Daniel 7:20)
- oratorical genius (Daniel 7:20)
- political genius (Daniel 11:21)
- commercial genius (Daniel 8:25)
- military genius (Daniel 8:24)
- administrative genius (Revelation 13:1-2)
- religious genius (2 Thessalonians 2:4)

Perhaps the most telling of his characteristics is depicted in Daniel 11:21, which tells us that he will come to power and "seize it through intrigue" ("flatteries," KJV). He will be a master of deception, empowered by the "father of lies." Many believe he will be Satan incarnate—thus his seemingly miraculous recovery in Revelation 13:3.

Notice the contrasts between Christ and the Antichrist. These include:

| Christ | Antichrist |
|:---:|:---:|
| the Truth | the Lie |
| Holy One | Lawless One |
| Man of Sorrows | Man of Sin |
| Son of God | Son of Satan |

| Christ | Antichrist |
|---|---|
| mystery of godliness | mystery of iniquity |
| Good Shepherd | Worthless Shepherd |
| exalted on high | cast down to hell |
| humbled Himself | exalted himself |
| despised | admired |
| cleanses the Temple | defiles the Temple |
| slain for the people | slays the people |
| the Lamb | the Beast |

A simple survey of the characteristics of the Antichrist confirms that he is both a false Christ (*pseudochristos*) and against Christ (*antichristos*). He masquerades as an angel of light only to plunge the world into spiritual darkness. Like Satan, he is a destroyer, not a builder. Promising peace, he pushes the world into war. In every conceivable way, he is just like Satan, who indwells and empowers him.

## Is the Antichrist Alive Today?

The spirit of Antichrist is alive and well! It is the Satan-inspired expression of lawlessness and rebellion against God, the things of God, and the people of God. It has been alive since Satan slithered his way around the Garden of Eden. It has been the driving force behind the whole terrible history of the human race—wars, murders, thefts, and rapes. It is the ugly expression of the destructive nature of the great deceiver himself.

The New Testament authors assure us that the spirit of Antichrist was active in their day over 20 centuries ago. It has remained active throughout the whole of church history, expressing itself in persecutions, heresies, spiritual deceptions, false prophets, and false religions. Satan has battled the church at every turn throughout its long history, waiting for the right moment to indwell the right person—the Antichrist—as his final masterpiece.

Attempting to guess whether certain contemporary figures might be the Antichrist, however, has always proven futile. Viewing the future through the eyes of the present led to some fantastic speculations about the identity of Antichrist in the past: Nero, Charlemagne, Napoleon, Mussolini, Hitler, Stalin, Gorbachev, and even Bill Clinton.

Jesus Himself said, "Of that day and hour no one knows, not even the angels of heaven, nor the Son, but My Father only" (Matthew 24:36). The obvious point of this passage is that no one knows the time, so there's no sense in trying to guess when Christ will return. It's far better that we be ready all the time because Jesus could come at any time!

Any apparent delay in Christ's return is not due to God's indecision, but to the fact that He has not let us in on the secret. Nor has He revealed this to Satan, who is a limited, finite being. Satan himself is left guessing when the rapture might occur. This means he must have a man in mind to indwell as the Antichrist in every generation. In other words, any one of a number of people could have been the Antichrist, but only one will be. Satan too must keep selecting candidates and waiting for God's timing.

The apostle Paul comments on this in 2 Thessalonians 2:1-12 when he tells us that the "coming of our Lord Jesus" (verse 1) will not happen until the "falling away comes first" and the "man of sin is revealed" (verse 3). He then tells us that "you know what is holding him back, so that he may be revealed at the proper time" (verse 6 NIV). Only after the rapture of the church will the identity of the Antichrist be revealed. In other words, you don't want to know who he is. If you ever do figure out who he is and you're still here on Earth, then you have been left behind!

Since Satan must prepare a man to be his crowning achievement in every generation, it should not surprise us that several likely candidates have appeared on the horizon of human history only to vanish away. Satan must wait on God's timing. He can't make his move until God releases the restraining power of the Holy Spirit indwelling the church. The Spirit is the agent and the church is the means by which God restrains Satan's diabolical plan—until the Father calls us home to heaven via the rapture.

In the meantime, Satan waits for his opportunity to destroy the whole world and the ultimate plan of God. He may be a defeated foe, but he has every intention of keeping up the fight to the very end. Even now he is moving about restlessly, searching for the right man to be the Antichrist.

## Ten Keys to Antichrist's Identity

The Bible gives us at least ten keys to identifying the Antichrist when he does come to power. They provide enough details to give a general idea of who he will be when Satan inspires him to make his move onto the world scene. These clues also make it clear that only one person in history will fit this description. There have been many prototypes, but there will be only one Antichrist.

1. *He will rise to power in the last days:* "...later in the time of wrath [the time of the end]....a stern-faced king, a master of intrigue, will arise" (Daniel 8:19,23 NIV).

2. *He will rule the whole world:* "Authority was given him over every tribe, tongue, and nation" (Revelation 13:7).

3. *His headquarters will be in Rome:* "The beast that you saw was, and is not, and will ascend out of the bottomless pit.... The seven heads are seven mountains on which the woman sits" (Revelation 17:8-9).

4. *He is intelligent and persuasive:* "The other horn...looked more imposing than the others and...had eyes and a mouth that spoke boastfully" (Daniel 7:20 NIV).

5. *He rules by international consent:* "The ten horns which you saw are ten kings.... These are of one mind, and will give their power and authority to the beast" (Revelation 17:12-13).

6. *He rules by deception:* "He will become very strong....and will succeed in whatever he does....He will cause deceit to prosper, and he will consider himself superior" (Daniel 8:24-25 NIV).

7. *He controls the global economy:* "He causes all, both small and great, rich and poor, free and slave, to receive a mark on their right hand or on their foreheads, and that no one may buy or sell except one who has the mark or name of the beast, or the number of his name" (Revelation 13:16-17).

8. *He will make a peace treaty with Israel:* "Then he shall confirm a covenant with many for one week; but in the middle of the week he shall bring an end to sacrifice and offering" (Daniel 9:27).

9. *He will break the treaty and invade Israel:* "The people of the prince who is to come shall destroy the city and the sanctuary. The end of it shall be with a flood, and till the end of the war desolations are determined" (Daniel 9:26).

10. *He will claim to be God:* "He will oppose and will exalt himself over everything that is called God or is worshiped, so that he sets himself up in God's temple, proclaiming himself to be God" (2 Thessalonians 2:4 NIV).

There are many other details given in the Bible regarding the person we commonly call the Antichrist. He will administrate the world government and the global economy, assisted by the leader of the world religion (Revelation 13:11-18). He may be moving into power at this very moment; only time will reveal his true identity.

When the Antichrist does come to power, he apparently will promise world peace through a series of international alliances, treaties, and agreements (see Daniel 8:24; Revelation 17:12). Despite his promises of peace, his international policies will inevitably plunge the world into the greatest war of all time. And at the end of the Tribulation, when Christ returns, the Antichrist will be destroyed. The good news for God's people is that he will not come to power until *after* the rapture.

## Lesson 6
# Rise of the Antichrist

Christians are often surprised to discover that there are more than 100 passages of Scripture that describe the Antichrist who will rise up in the last days. While the term *Antichrist* itself is used very little in the Bible, the Antichrist and the global system he runs are mentioned numerous times.

Through the ages, many people have tried to identify this coming world ruler, but the Bible simply does not give us enough information to make this determination. Instead, we are given some general clues and facts—and it's important that we use discernment and keep these facts separated from the rampant speculation that often occurs in an attempt to figure out who the Antichrist is.

1.  On pages 50-51 are 11 different titles the Bible uses to speak of the Antichrist. With reference to these titles, what are some general conclusions you can make about the character of this person?

2.  According to the explanation on page 52, what is significant about the prefix anti in the name Antichrist?

3.  Read 2 Thessalonians 2:4. What will the Antichrist oppose? Where will he do this? What will he proclaim about himself?

4.  Yet what does God say in Isaiah 45:5-6 about anyone who might try to oppose Him?

5.  In Revelation 19:19, we're told the Antichrist ("the beast") will attempt to make war against the Lord. According to verse 20, what will happen to the Antichrist?

6.  Read Revelation 13:7. What will be the extent of Antichrist's authority during his reign?

7. What do we read about the extent of God's authority in...

> 1 Chronicles 29:11-12—
>
> Psalm 10:16—
>
> Revelation 19:16—

## Applying Prophecy to Everyday Life

While it's true the Antichrist will wield enormous power and unleash unimaginable cruelty upon the world, we do not need to be fearful of Him. The outcome is already certain—Jesus will defeat the Antichrist upon His return, and we will reign with Jesus' kingdom on earth. How does this knowledge comfort or encourage you?

# 7

# BEWARE OF FALSE PROPHETS

The Antichrist will not rise to power alone; his success will result from a worldwide spiritual deception perpetrated by an associate, the False Prophet, who is also known as the second "beast" (Revelation 13:11-17). This so-called prophet's ability to perform miraculous signs will enable him to convince people that the Antichrist is the leader for whom they have been looking. The False Prophet will also encourage worldwide worship of the Antichrist (Revelation 19:20; 20:10). In Scripture the False Prophet's identity is not revealed, but Revelation 13 presents ten identifying features that help us to know who he is. The False Prophet...

1. rises out of the earth (13:11)
2. is motivated by Satan (13:11)
3. controls religious affairs (13:12)
4. promotes the worship of the beast (13:12)
5. performs signs and miracles (13:13)
6. deceives the whole world (13:14)

7. empowers the image of the beast (13:15)
8. kills all who refuse to worship (13:15)
9. controls all economic commerce (13:17)
10. controls the mark of the beast (13:17-18)

Bible scholars are divided on whether the False Prophet will be Jewish or Gentile. The biblical record itself is inconclusive on this matter. However, when we observe the relationship of the False Prophet to the great prostitute (Revelation 17), we immediately notice his connection to the city on "seven mountains" (see 17:7,9) that rules "over the kings of the earth" (verse 18). It seems clear that John is referring to Rome by the terminology he uses to describe the symbol of "Babylon the Great" (verse 5).

Ironically, little has been written about the False Prophet compared to the volumes of material about the Antichrist. The Antichrist and the False Prophet are two separate individuals who will work toward a common, deceptive goal. Their roles and relationship will be similar to that which was common in the ancient world between a ruler (Antichrist) and the high priest (False Prophet) of a national religion.

## Work of the False Prophet

The False Prophet is depicted in Revelation as one who uses miraculous signs and wonders to deceive the world into worshiping the Antichrist. The False Prophet will extend his ecclesiastical administration over the whole earth by establishing the church of the Antichrist, which is a counterfeit of the true church.

This apostate religion will be bound together by a common hatred of genuine Christianity. Thus, the False Prophet does not so much deny Christian doctrine as he corrupts it. Only in this way can the Antichrist sit in the temple of God, demanding to be worshiped as God (2 Thessalonians 2:4; see also Isaiah 14:12-14). Remember, when Satan tempted Christ, he appealed for worship (Matthew 4:8-10). In fact, Satan offered to surrender the entire world to Christ if He would worship him. Therefore, it should not surprise us that the goal of the Satan-inspired False Prophet will be to get the whole world to bow down to the Antichrist, who is the personification of Satan himself.

Together, Satan (the dragon), Antichrist (the beast of the sea), and the False Prophet (the beast of the earth) will comprise an "unholy trinity" that is a counterfeit of the triune God. Generally speaking, Satan opposes the Father, Antichrist opposes the Son, and the False Prophet opposes the Holy Spirit. This ungodly alliance will be Satan's final attempt to overthrow the work of God on earth.

The method of this alliance's diabolical attempt is explained in the biblical record. The Antichrist dare not appear until after removal of the Restrainer and the resulting "rebellion" (NIV) or "falling away" (KJV) of apostasy. In the meantime, the spirit of Antichrist (lawlessness) is already at work attempting to pervert the gospel and corrupt the true church. When this process is sufficiently established, the False Prophet will arise to prepare for the coming of the Antichrist.

The False Prophet is depicted as having "two horns like a lamb, but he spoke like a dragon" (Revelation 13:11). He looks religious, but he talks like the devil. He counterfeits true religion in order to hide his real identity. Just as the Holy Spirit is dedicated to bringing the world to know Jesus Christ, the False Prophet is dedicated to bringing all men into spiritual allegiance with the Antichrist.

It should not surprise us then that the False Prophet represents the apostate religion of the end times. If his rise to power parallels that of the Antichrist, he will preside over apostate Christendom after the rapture of true believers to heaven. All that are left behind—no matter what their religious affiliation—will be spiritually blind unbelievers. In such an environment, the False Prophet will have no problem deceiving the whole world. While the Holy Spirit will still be omnipresent in the world, the removal of the church (the body of Christ) will bring His restraining ministry to an end.

## The Great Lie

The apostle Paul explained this process when he wrote: "For the secret power of lawlessness is already at work; but the one who now holds it back will continue to do so till he is taken out of the way" (2 Thessalonians 2:7 NIV). After the rapture, the Holy Spirit will still convict people of sin, but His restraining ministry will be over and all of Satan's evil will break loose on Earth. Then the lawless one will be revealed. Paul said, "The coming of the lawless one will be in accordance with the work of Satan displayed in all kinds of counterfeit miracles, signs and wonders, and in every sort of evil that deceives those who are perishing" (2 Thessalonians 2:9-10 NIV). The rise of the Antichrist will correspond with a general breakdown in religious and moral values, resulting in a decadent society that will believe "the lie" rather than the truth. The apostle Paul does not define "the lie," but he specifies that it is a particular lie, not just any lie. It is possible that this could refer to a falsehood perpetrated to explain away the rapture (for example, those who disappeared were abducted by aliens). But it is more likely that the lie is the official rejection of Christ and the acceptance of the deification and worship of the Antichrist.

The False Prophet is presented in Revelation as an individual who is empowered by Satan (13:11-12). The religious system that he represents is called the "great harlot" (17:1) who is drunk with the "blood of the saints" (17:6). Therefore, the final phase of apostasy is both a religious system and the individual who leads it.

## The Master of Deceit

The Bible describes Satan as the "father of lies" (John 8:44 NIV) and pictures him as the ultimate deceiver. His name means "accuser," and he is depicted as the accuser of God and His people (Revelation 12:10). He is opposed to God and seeks to alienate people from the truth. He misled the fallen angels (Revelation 12:3-4), and tempts men and women to sin against God's laws (Genesis 3:1-13; 1 Timothy 6:9). He denies and rejects the truth of God and deceives those who perish without God

(2 Thessalonians 2:10). Ultimately, he inspires the false prophets and the very spirit of the Antichrist (1 John 2:18-23).

The Bible clearly warns us that in the last days people will "abandon the faith and follow deceiving ['seducing,' KJV] spirits and things ['doctrines,' KJV] taught by demons" (1 Timothy 4:1 NIV). These false teachings will come through hypocritical liars whose minds have been captured by Satan's lies (1 Timothy 4:2). So the False Prophet will not be alone in his deception; there will be many other false prophets in the last days.

What are the characteristics of false prophets? How can we recognize them? The Bible describes them in these ways:

> *Self-deceived.* Some false teachers may be sincere, but because their message is wrong, they themselves are wrong. They have deceived themselves into believing that their false messages are true. Their messages come from within their own minds and are not from God.
>
> *Liars.* Some false prophets are deliberate liars who have no intention of telling the truth. The apostle John says, "Who is a liar but he who denies that Jesus is the Christ? He is antichrist who denies the Father and the Son" (1 John 2:22).
>
> *Heretics.* These are people who preach heresy (false doctrine) and divide the church. Of them John said, "They went out from us, but they were not of us" (1 John 2:19). The apostle Peter said, "There will be false teachers among you, who will secretly bring in destructive heresies.... [These men] speak evil of the things they do not understand" (2 Peter 2:1,12).
>
> *Scoffers.* There are some who do not necessarily promote false teaching so much as they outright reject the truth of God. Of them the Bible warns, "Scoffers will come in the last days, walking according to their own lusts" (2 Peter 3:3). The apostle Paul calls them "lovers of themselves...boasters,

proud...haughty" (2 Timothy 3:2,4). Jude calls them "grumblers, complainers" (verse 16).

*Blasphemers.* Those who speak evil of God, Christ, the Holy Spirit, the people of God, the kingdom of God, and the attributes of God are called blasphemers. Jude calls them godless men who "speak abusively against whatever they do not understand....They are clouds without rain...trees, without fruit...wild waves of the sea...wandering stars" (verses 10,12-13 NIV). The apostle Paul said that he himself was a blasphemer before his conversion to Christ (1 Timothy 1:13).

*Seducers.* Jesus warned that some false prophets will perform miraculous signs and wonders to seduce or deceive the very elect "if possible" (Mark 13:22). Our Lord's implication is that spiritual seduction is a very real threat even to believers. This would account for the fact that a few genuine, but deceived, believers may be found among the cults.

*Reprobates.* This term means "disapproved," "depraved," or "rejected." In Romans chapter 1 Paul refers to those who have rejected the truth of God and turned to spiritual darkness. Consequently, God has given them over to a "reprobate mind" (verse 28 KJV). They have so deliberately rejected God that they have become "filled with all unrighteousness" (verse 29). As a result, they are "haters of God" (verse 30), whose behavior is "undiscerning, untrustworthy, unloving, unforgiving" (verse 31). These people are so far gone spiritually that they know it and don't care.

In Jesus' prophetic Olivet Discourse (Matthew 24–25), He warned, "Take heed that no one deceives you....many will be offended...many false prophets will rise up and deceive many....false christs and false prophets will rise and show great signs and wonders" (Matthew 24:4,10-11,24). Our Lord warned His disciples—and us—of the possibility of spiritual seduction by false prophets and teachers, especially as the end of the age approaches.

Spiritual deception is the goal of the False Prophet as he encourages people to embrace the social, economic, and religious program of the Antichrist. These sweeping changes will be able to occur rapidly with the help of television and the Internet. As we approach the end of the age, then, we can fully expect that false prophets and spiritual darkness will engulf the world.

# Beware of False Prophets

The Antichrist, in his bid to rule the world, will have the help of "the second beast," or the False Prophet, who is described in Revelation 13:11-17. This False Prophet's main role will be to give the Antichrist an appearance of credibility, to deceive the world into worshiping the Antichrist.

Little is written in the Bible about the False Prophet himself, but a lot is said about the danger of false prophets in general. As we consider the Bible's warnings, we can come to appreciate the enormous seriousness of what the False Prophet will do during the last days.

1.  What did Jesus say about the outward appearance and true inner nature of false prophets in Matthew 7:15?

2.  According to the apostle Paul in 2 Timothy 4:3-4, what will people turn away from, and listen to instead?

3.  How are false teachers described in Ephesians 4:14?

4.  Read 2 Peter 2:1-3. What three things will false prophets do, according to verse 1? How will they do this (see verse 3)?

5.  Read 2 Peter 2:12-17. What are some ways Peter describes false prophets? Why do you think Peter uses such strong language?

## *Applying Prophecy to Everyday Life*

What are some ways we can protect ourselves against false teachers, according to…

2 Peter 3:14—

2 Peter 3:18—

2 Timothy 3:10,14-17—

8

# THE TRIBULATION PERIOD

Jesus warned His disciples that in the last days there would be a period of time more horrific and traumatic than any other time in human history. He was, of course, referring to the Great Tribulation:

> There will be great tribulation, such as has not been since the beginning of the world until this time, no, nor ever shall be (Matthew 24:21).

The disciples were familiar with this prophesied time of anguish, for many of the Hebrew prophets of old had warned Israel about a future period of intense suffering. The prophet Jeremiah called it "the time of Jacob's trouble" (Jeremiah 30:7). Throughout the Old and New Testaments, the Tribulation is referred to by a variety of names including "the day of the Lord" (1 Thessalonians 5:2), the seventieth week of Daniel (Daniel 9:27), "a day of desolation" (Zephaniah 1:15), "the wrath to come" (1 Thessalonians 1:10), "the hour of judgment" (Revelation 14:7), and "the great tribulation" (Matthew 24:21). Not only is the Tribulation mentioned in more than 60 passages in the Bible, but more space is allotted to it than any other subject except for salvation and the second coming of Christ.

# THE TRIBULATION IN CONTEXT

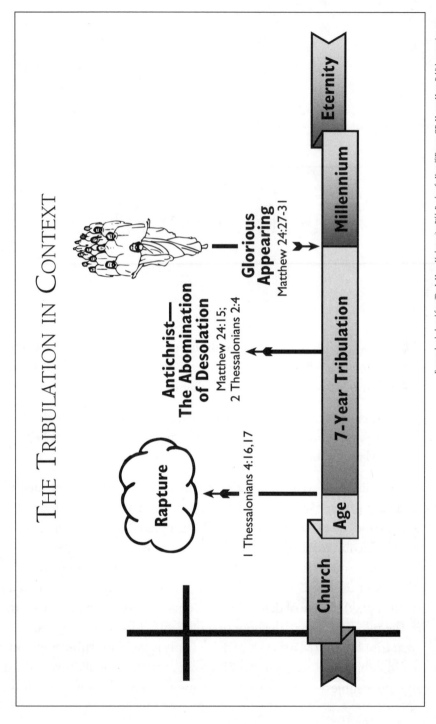

**Rapture**
1 Thessalonians 4:16,17

**Antichrist—
The Abomination
of Desolation**
Matthew 24:15;
2 Thessalonians 2:4

**Glorious
Appearing**
Matthew 24:27-31

Church

Age

7-Year Tribulation

Millennium

Eternity

Excerpted and adapted from Tim LaHaye, *Understanding Bible Prophecy for Yourself* (Eugene, OR: Harvest House Publishers, 2001), p. 135.

Both the prophet Daniel and the apostle John stated this period would last seven years (Daniel 9:24-27; Revelation 11:2-3). After rising to power, the evil "prince who is to come" (Daniel 9:26), the Antichrist, will make a covenant with Israel. This event will signal the beginning of the seven-year Tribulation period. Three and a half years into the Tribulation, at the halfway point, the Antichrist will break the covenant by desecrating the rebuilt Temple in Jerusalem. This will usher in the Great Tribulation, a period of suffering and terror worse than any that mankind has ever experienced in history. Although the Tribulation lasts only seven years, the devastations unleashed during that time will seem endless to those who must face them.

## The Nature of the Tribulation

Through various prophetic passages found in the Bible, we learn that the Tribulation will be...

- a time of *judgment* for those who reject the Savior
- a time of *conclusion* for those who rebel against God
- a time of *decision* for those who will be forced to choose between Christ and the Antichrist
- a time of *chaos* designed to shake mankind's false sense of security
- a time of unprecedented *revival,* resulting in the greatest soul harvest in history

When will the Tribulation take place? Although no exact date is given, the Bible indicates in Matthew 24:29-31 that it must occur immediately before the glorious appearing of Christ, when Jesus Himself returns to Earth to destroy the Antichrist. It will also occur after the rapture of the church, when all those who have placed their trust in Jesus Christ will be instantly removed from the planet in order to meet the Lord in the air (1 Thessalonians 4:15-18).

Those who view the Tribulation as primarily a time of wrath overlook the fact that it is also a time of mercy and grace. The Lord is not some angry monster heaping catastrophes upon the heads of innocent men and women. In reality, the people who suffer the judgments of God during the Tribulation are not innocent. Not only do these rebels reject God and His free offer of salvation, they indulge in every vile sin known to mankind, including the massacre of those who come to Christ during this time. Even then, God's hope is that these rebels will at some point turn to Him. The Tribulation judgments therefore serve a dual purpose: to punish hardened sinners, and to move others to repentance. The following Scripture passage exemplifies this truth:

> I will show wonders in the heavens and in the earth: Blood and fire and pillars of smoke. The sun shall be turned into darkness, and the moon into blood, before the coming of the great and awesome day of the LORD. And it shall come to pass that whoever calls on the name of the LORD shall be saved (Joel 2:30-32).

## The Tribulation Saints

The untold millions who miss the rapture because of their rejection of God will still have an opportunity to become saved. The apostle John writes...

> After these things I looked, and behold, a great multitude which no one could number, of all nations, tribes, peoples, and tongues, standing before the throne and before the Lamb, clothed with white robes, with palm branches in their hands (Revelation 7:9).

These Tribulation saints, whose numbers are so large they can't be counted, come to the Lord as a result of the Tribulation's trials—demonstrating that our holy God is a God who will continue to show His love and mercy to mankind even in the last days. When John asked, "Who is this great multitude?" the reply was "These are the ones who come out of the great tribulation" (Revelation 7:14). No wonder the apostle Peter was able to write, "The Lord is not slack concerning His promise, as some count slackness, but is longsuffering toward us, not willing that any should perish but that all should come to repentance" (2 Peter 3:9).

## Those Left Behind

In many respects, the rapture will set the stage for the coming Tribulation. Following the disappearance of millions upon millions of Christians from the face of the Earth, the world will be in a state of shock and chaos that defies comprehension. This will prepare the way perfectly for the rise of the Antichrist. He will come to power peaceably using diplomacy—as represented by the rider on the white horse, the first of the four horsemen of the Apocalypse (Revelation 6:1-2). His charm and outward compassion will bring badly needed comfort to a populace on the brink of mass hysteria.

The controlled media will be used to effectively coerce the world into adopting this new leader as the man of the hour. Ongoing efforts to discredit the Bible and other prophetic books such as the *Left Behind* series, which foretold the rapture and the rise of the Antichrist in advance, will be a top priority of the new world government. Every attempt will be made to convince the confused populace that those who have been left behind are, in fact, the lucky ones, even though nothing could be further from the truth.

The spiritual vacuum left by the disappearance of millions of Christians will also enable the Antichrist to further his plan for a forced one-world religion. This pagan religion will unite all religions—with the lone exception of biblical Christianity—into one. In the midst of all this, the Holy Spirit will work through the 144,000 evangelists and the two witnesses in Jerusalem to draw countless numbers of people to Christ during the Tribulation—despite the fact that such a choice will most likely result in martyrdom.

## World War III

After his peaceful ascension to power, the Antichrist will initiate what we might call World War III (Revelation 6:3-4) against three of the ten regional leaders who will be in power during this time. Death and destruction will be brought to this earth on a massive scale never before known. This battle may involve a nuclear exchange and will be followed by widespread inflation, famine, and disease. Possibly due in part to nuclear fallout, plagues will sweep across the land and death will come to a fourth of the world's population (Revelation 6:5-8). All the while, the Antichrist will be carrying out his vengeance against those who have chosen to follow Christ instead of him (Revelation 6:9-11). And the killing of millions of Tribulation saints will escalate as the world sinks further into death and despair.

Up to this point, the judgments that have come upon Earth during the Tribulation are largely the result of man's endeavors. From here onward, however, the judgments will be acts of divine retribution. Revelation 6:12-15 describes a massive earthquake so large that "every mountain and island was moved out of its place" (verse 14). Apparently there will be a series of massive volcanic eruptions as well, which will cause the sky to darken and the moon to appear red. The apostle John also writes of meteor-like objects that come crashing down onto the earth. So incredible are these events that Earth's inhabitants will realize they are witnessing God's judgments right before their eyes:

> The kings of the earth, the great men, the rich men, the commanders, the mighty men, every slave and every free man, hid themselves in the caves and in the rocks of the mountains, and said to the mountains and rocks, "Fall on us and hide us from the face of Him who sits on the throne and from the wrath of the Lamb! For the great day of His wrath has come, and who is able to stand?" (Revelation 6:15-17).

Then hail, fire, and blood will rain down from the sky, causing a third of the earth's trees and grass to burn up. Two more meteors will fall from the sky and kill a third of the sea life, destroy a third of the ships at sea, and poison a third of the earth's fresh water supply. Darkness will continue to envelope the land as the light from the sun and moon is dimmed by a third.

## Hell on Earth

Revelation chapter 9 describes a plague of locust-like creatures that descend upon the earth and have the ability to sting people. For five months, these creatures will torment, but not kill, unbelievers:

> Out of the smoke locusts came upon the earth. And to them was given power, as the scorpions of the earth have power. They were commanded not to harm the grass of the earth, or any green thing, or any tree, but only those men who do not have the seal of God on their foreheads. And they were not given authority to kill them, but to torment them for five months. Their torment was like the torment of a scorpion when it strikes a man. In those days men will seek death and will not find it; they will desire to die, and death will flee from them (Revelation 9:3-6).

If that weren't enough, armies of demonic horsemen will then be unleashed and kill another third of the world's population (Revelation 9:13-19).

And then it gets worse…

## The Mark of the Beast

As mentioned previously, halfway into the Tribulation, the Antichrist will break his treaty with the nation of Israel, desecrate the rebuilt Temple in Jerusalem, and kill the two witnesses who have been proclaiming the gospel (Revelation 11:3-12). He will then seize total control over the monetary system of the world (Revelation 13:16-18), requiring all to carry his mark, which in some way will consist of the number 666. This is the prophesied mark of the beast, and without it, no one will be able to buy or sell: "He causes all, both small and great, rich and poor, free and slave, to receive a mark on their right hand or on their foreheads, and that no one may buy or sell except one who has the mark" (Revelation 13:16-17).

Even a few short years ago, such a prospect would have seemed inconceivable. But now, with computerized electronic deposit/debit transfers occurring on a worldwide scale, the ability to control and track the purchases of every human being is not only possible, but inevitable.

## Preparing for Armageddon

Meanwhile, as the Tribulation progresses, the judgments of God will continue to afflict the ungodly. Loathsome sores will break out upon those who have the mark of the beast. The sea and remaining fresh water will be turned into blood. Heat from the sun will scorch the unrepentant, and darkness will envelope the kingdom of the Antichrist (Revelation 16:2-11).

Then the Euphrates River will dry up, allowing the armies of the east to march unhindered to Israel to begin the Battle of Armageddon. The bloodshed will reach unparalleled proportions. A tremendous earthquake will level the cities of the world, and hailstones weighing as much as 100 pounds will fall to the earth. Unfortunately, many of the ungodly still will not repent, despite the severity of these judgments:

> There was a great earthquake, such a mighty and great earthquake as had not occurred since men were on the earth. Now the great city was divided into three parts, and the cities of the nations fell. And great Babylon was remembered before God, to give her the cup of the wine of the fierceness of His wrath. Then every island fled away, and the mountains were not found. And great hail from heaven fell upon men, each hailstone about the weight of a talent. Men blasphemed God because of the plague of the hail, since that plague was exceedingly great (Revelation 16:18-21).

And with that, the judgments will draw to an end. The glorious appearing of Christ comes next. He will be in the air accompanied by the armies of heaven, which consist of all those who were raptured to heaven (Revelation 19:11-14). Christ will then descend to Earth in power and glory to win the Battle of Armageddon. He will cast the beast (Antichrist) and False Prophet into the Lake of Fire, and bind Satan in the abyss for 1000 years. Then He will initiate His millennial reign on earth (Revelation 19:19–20:3).

# The Tribulation Period

"You ain't seen nothin' yet" is a phrase that could aptly be used to describe the Tribulation. The horrors of this future time of judgment will be of a magnitude far beyond any cataclysmic event that has ever taken place in history. Even the most widespread and devastating of wars to date will pale by comparison to all that happens during the Tribulation, which will culminate in the war of all wars, Armageddon.

The Bible affirms the tremendous significance of the Tribulation by giving it a lot of attention. More is said about this seven-year period of wrath than about the 1000-year millennial kingdom, heaven, or hell. We find mention of it in the Old Testament at least 49 times, and at least 15 times in the New Testament.

1. The Tribulation is referred to by many names in the Bible. What names or descriptive phrases are used in these passages?

    Isaiah 34:8—

    Daniel 12:1—

    Zephaniah 1:15—

    Revelation 3:10—

2. Taken together, what do the aforementioned verses teach you about the nature of the Tribulation?

3. In the book of Daniel, in relation to the Tribulation, the term "week" refers to seven years. What will initiate this "week," or the Tribulation, according to Daniel 9:27?

4. What will happen at the middle of the seven-year Tribulation (see Daniel 9:27; Matthew 24:15)?

5.  What will occur at the end of the Tribulation (see Revelation 19:11-21)?

6.  The Tribulation will not merely be a time of judgment, but also one last clarion call for the lost to receive Jesus Christ as their Savior. Briefly describe the instruments God will use to spread the gospel during this time:

    Revelation 7:4-8—

    Revelation 11:3—

    Revelation 14:6-7—

## *Applying Prophecy to Everyday Life*

The people who are saved during the Tribulation will comprise "a great multitude which no one could number" (Revelation 7:9). Indeed, in the midst of the extreme horrors of the Tribulation, God will call to Himself many, many more people—a testimony of just how loving and merciful He is, giving people ample opportunity to repent of their sins.

Do you have a compassion for the lost? Who could you be praying for, or reaching out to with the message of salvation in Christ?

# 9

# THE GLORIOUS APPEARING

The second coming of Christ is the most anticipated event in human history. The "glorious appearing" (Titus 2:13) is the ultimate fulfillment of our Lord's promise to return. It is also the culmination of all biblical prophecy. The return of Christ is the final apologetic! Once He returns, there will be no further need to debate His claims or the validity of the Christian message. The King will come in person to set the record straight.

Revelation 19 is probably the most dramatic chapter in all the Bible. It is the capstone to the death and resurrection of Christ. In this chapter we see the living Savior return to Earth to crush all satanic opposition to the truth. He will establish His kingdom on earth in fulfillment of the Old Testament prophecies and of His own promise to return.

Just before the crucifixion, the disciples asked Jesus, "What will be the sign of Your coming, and of the end of the age?" (Matthew 24:3). Our Lord replied, "Immediately after the tribulation of those days...the powers of the heavens will be shaken. Then the sign of the Son of Man will appear in heaven, and then all the tribes of the earth will mourn, and they will see the Son of Man coming on the clouds of heaven with power and great glory" (Matthew 24:29-30).

As Jesus looked down the corridor of time to the end of the present age, He warned of a time of great tribulation that would come upon the whole world (Matthew 24:5-28). Our Lord went on to explain that the devastation that takes place will be so extensive that unless those days were cut short, "no flesh would be saved" (Matthew 24:22). Jesus further described this coming day of trouble as a time when the sun and moon will be darkened and "the powers of the heavens will be shaken" (Matthew 24:29). His description runs parallel to that found in Revelation 16:1-16, where the final hour of the Tribulation is depicted by atmospheric darkness, air pollution, and ecological disaster.

The return of Christ will mark both the total defeat of the Antichrist and the total triumph of Christ. Without Christ, there is no hope of a better future. He is the central figure of the world to come. It is His kingdom, and we are His bride.

## The Promise of Christ's Return

Jesus promised His disciples, in the upper room, that He was going to heaven to prepare a place for them. Then He said, "If I go and prepare a place for you, I will come again, and receive you unto myself; that where I am, there ye may be also" (John 14:3 KJV). Even though the early disciples eventually died, the Bible promised, "Behold I show you a mystery; we shall not all sleep [die], but we shall all be changed [resurrected or raptured], in a moment, in the twinkling of an eye, at the last trump: for the trumpet shall sound, and the dead shall be raised incorruptible, and we shall be changed" (1 Corinthians 15:51-52 KJV).

The apostle Paul reiterates this same hope in 1 Thessalonians 4:13-17, where he comments about those believers who have already died and gone to heaven. He says, "If we believe that Jesus died and rose again, even so them also which sleep [die] in Jesus will God bring with him [from heaven]....For the Lord himself shall descend from heaven with a shout, with the voice of the archangel, and with the trump of God: and the dead in Christ shall rise first: then we who are alive and remain shall be caught up together with them in the clouds to meet the Lord in the air" (verses 14-17).

The promise to return for the church (believers of the church age) is a promise of the rapture. Jesus' specific promise to return personally and physically to take His church up to heaven guarantees that fact! When Revelation 19 opens the church is already in heaven with Christ at the marriage supper. The rapture has already occurred. Jesus is depicted as the groom and the church as the bride. The marriage supper celebrates their union after the rapture and before their return to Earth.

One of the greatest interpretive problems for nonrapturists is to explain *how* the church got to heaven *prior* to the second coming! Surely they are not all martyred, or else Paul's comment about "we who are alive and remain" (1 Thessalonians 4:15) would be meaningless. The rapture must be presumed to have occurred *before* the events in Revelation 19—amillennialists and postmillennialists notwithstanding!

The position of the church (bride of the Lamb) in Revelation 19:7-10 *in heaven* is crucial to the interpretation of the entire apocalypse. The church is not mentioned during the seal, trumpet, and bowl judgments because the church is not on Earth during the outpouring of these judgments. The term "church" (Greek, *ekklesia*) appears frequently in Revelation chapters 1–3. In fact, it is used 19 times in those chapters. But the word "church" does not appear again until Revelation 22:16. In the meantime, the church appears in Revelation 19:7-10 as the bride of the Lamb.

The concept of the church as the bride or wife of Christ is clearly stated in Ephesians 5:25-26, where husbands are admonished to love their wives as Christ loved the church and gave Himself for her that He might present her in heaven as a glorious bride. There can be no doubt, therefore, that John intends us to see the Lamb's "wife" as the church—the bride of Christ.

## The Nature of Christ's Return

Jesus not only promised to return for His church; He also promised to return to judge the world and to establish His kingdom on earth. His half-brother James refers to believers as "heirs of the kingdom which He promised to those who love him" (James 2:5). Jesus Himself told His disciples that He would not drink the fruit of the vine after the last supper until He drank it with them in His Father's kingdom (Matthew 26:29). After the resurrection, the disciples asked Jesus, "Will You at this time restore the kingdom to Israel?" (Acts 1:6). Jesus replied that the time was in the Father's hand. All these references imply a future kingdom when Christ returns.

The details of Christ's return are as follows:

1. *He will return personally.* The Bible says that "the Lord Himself will descend from heaven" (1 Thessalonians 4:16). Jesus promised He will return in person (Matthew 24:30).

2. *He will appear as the Son of Man.* Since Pentecost, Christ has ministered through the Holy Spirit (John 14:16-23; 16:7-20). But when He returns, He will appear as the Son of Man in His glorified human form (Matthew 24:30; 26:64; see also Daniel 7:13-14).

3. *He will return literally and visibly.* In Acts 1:11 the angels promised, "This same Jesus, who was taken up from you into heaven, will so come in like manner." Revelation 1:7 tells us, "Every eye will see him, even they who pierced him. And all the tribes of the earth will mourn." Nowhere in Scripture is there a suggestion that Christ's second coming in power and great glory will be anything but visible and physical. In fact, all unbelievers on the earth at the time of Christ's return will be eyewitnesses to it. Preterists, who claim Christ has already returned, cannot point to a time when anyone has ever witnessed such.

4. *He will come suddenly and dramatically.* Paul warned, "The day of the Lord so comes as a thief in the night" (1 Thessalonians 5:2). Jesus said, "For as the lightning comes from the east and flashes to the west so also will the coming of the Son of Man be" (Matthew 24:27).

5. *He will come on the clouds of heaven.* Jesus said, "They will see the Son of Man coming on the clouds of heaven" (Matthew 24:30). Daniel 7:13 makes the same prediction. So does Luke 21:27. Revelation 1:7 says, "Behold, He is coming with clouds."

6. *He will come in a display of glory.* Matthew 16:27 promises, "The Son of Man will come in the glory of His Father." Matthew 24:30 adds, "They will see the Son of Man coming…with power and great glory."

7. *He will come with all His angels.* Jesus promised He would "send His angels with a great sound of a trumpet" (Matthew 24:31). He said in one of His parables, "The reapers are the angels….so it will be at the end of this age" (Matthew 13:39-40).

8. *He will come with His bride, the church.* That, of course, is the whole point of Revelation 19. Colossians 3:4 adds, "When Christ…appears, then you also will appear with him in glory." Zechariah 14:5 says, "The Lord my God will come, and all the saints with You."

9. *He will return to the Mount of Olives.* "In that day His feet will stand on the Mount of Olives" (Zechariah 14:4). Where the glory of God ascended into heaven, it will return (Ezekiel 11:23). Where Jesus ascended into heaven, He will return (Acts 1:9-11).

10. *He will return in triumph and victory.* Zechariah 14:9 states, "The Lord shall be King over all the earth." Revelation 19:16 depicts him as "King of kings and Lord of lords." He will triumph over the Antichrist, the false prophet, and Satan (Revelation 19:19-21).

Revelation 19 opens with a heavenly chorus of "a great multitude" singing the praises of God (verse 1). The heavenly choir rejoices with praise because justice has finally been served. "True and righteous are his judgments," they sing, "because he has judged the great harlot"

(Revelation 19:2). The praise chorus then breaks into a fourfold "alleluia" in verses 1-6:

1. "Alleluia! Salvation and glory and power belong to the Lord our God" (verse 1).
2. "Alleluia! Her smoke rises up forever and ever!" (verse 3).
3. They "worshiped God…on the throne, saying, 'Amen! Alleluia!'" (verse 4).
4. "Alleluia! For the Lord God Omnipotent reigns!" (verse 6).

## The Marriage upon Christ's Return

The marriage of the Lamb is announced suddenly and dramatically. It is as though we have finally arrived at what we have been waiting for all along. The wedding is finally here. It is obvious that John the revelator views this as a future (not past) event. The church is the betrothed bride of Christ *now*, but our marriage to Him is in the future.

This is why we cannot say that the consummation of the marriage has already taken place. The apostle Paul writes, "For I have betrothed you to one husband, that I may present you as a chaste virgin to Christ" (2 Corinthians 11:2). He also adds that Christ "loved the church and gave Himself for her…that he might present her to Himself a glorious church, not having spot or wrinkle or any such thing, but that she should be holy and without blemish" (Ephesians 5:25-27).

The New Testament pictures the church as engaged to Christ at this present time. We are still awaiting the "judgment seat of Christ" (2 Corinthians 5:10), presumably after the rapture and before the marriage supper. The marriage ceremony itself will follow in heaven during the tribulation period on earth.

While Revelation 19 pictures Christ symbolically as the Lamb (verse 7), the picture of the marriage is clearly expressed. The aorist tense of "has come" (Greek, *elthen*) indicates a completed act, showing that the wedding is now consummated. Instead of the normal seven-day Jewish wedding ceremony, this one presumably lasts seven years (during the

Tribulation period). The marriage is completed in heaven (Revelation 19:7), but the marriage supper will probably take place later on Earth, where Israel is awaiting the return of Christ and the church.

This is the only way to distinguish the Bridegroom (Christ), the bride (church), and the ten virgins (Israel) in Matthew 25:1-13. There is no way that He is coming to marry all ten (or five) of these women. They are the attendants (Old Testament saints and Tribulation saints) at the wedding. Only the church is the bride. That is why Jesus could say of John the Baptist that there was not a "greater prophet" (Old Testament saint), but he that is "least in the kingdom of God" (New Testament church) is "greater than he" (Luke 7:28).

## The Triumph of Christ's Return

The picture of Christ's return in Revelation 19:11-16 is the most dramatic passage in all the Bible! In these six verses we are swept up into the triumphal entourage of redeemed saints as they ride in the heavenly procession with the King of kings and Lord of lords. In this one passage alone, all the hopes and dreams of every believer are finally and fully realized. This is not the Palm Sunday procession with the humble Messiah on the donkey colt. This is the ultimate in eschatological drama. The rejected Savior returns in triumph as the rightful King of all the world—and *we* are with Him.

The description of the triumphant Savior is that of a king leading an army to victory. The passage itself is the final phase of the seventh bowl of judgment begun in Revelation 16:17-21, moving through the details of 17:1–18:24 and on to chapter 19.

As the scene unfolds, heaven opens to reveal Christ followed by the army of the redeemed. The description of their being clad in white (verse 14) emphasizes the garments of the bride already mentioned earlier (verse 8). In this vignette, the bride appears as the army of the Messiah. But unlike contemporary apocalyptic dramas of that time (e.g., War Scroll of the Qumran sect), the victory is won without any military help from the faithful. This army has no weapons, no swords, no shields, no armor.

They are merely clad in the "righteous acts of the saints" (verse 8). They have not come to fight, but to watch. They have not come to assist, but to celebrate. The Messiah-King will do the fighting. He alone will win the battle by the power of His spoken word.

The *twelvefold description* of the coming King combines elements of symbolism from various biblical passages and from the other pictures of the risen Christ in the book of Revelation. Notice the details of His appearance:

1.  He rides the white horse (Revelation 6:2).
2.  He is called faithful and true (Revelation 3:14).
3.  He judges and makes war in righteousness (2 Thessalonians 1:7-8).
4.  His eyes are as a flame of fire (Revelation 1:14).
5.  He wears many crowns (Revelation 4:10).
6.  His name is unknown—a wonderful secret (Judges 13:18; Isaiah 9:6).
7.  He is clothed in a robe dipped in blood (Isaiah 63:1-6).
8.  His name is called the Word of God (John 1:1).
9.  A sharp sword is in His mouth (Revelation 19:15).
10. He rules with a rod of iron (Psalm 2:9).
11. He treads the winepress of the wrath of God (Isaiah 63:1-6; Revelation 14:14-20).
12. His written name is King of kings and Lord of lords (Daniel 2:47; Revelation 17:14).

There can be no doubt that in Revelation 19:11-16, the rider on the white horse is Jesus Christ. He comes as the apostle Paul predicted: "in flaming fire taking vengeance on those who do not know God.... [who] shall be punished with everlasting destruction...when He comes, in that Day, to be glorified in His saints and to be admired among all those who believe" (2 Thessalonians 1:8-10).

This is the true Christ (Messiah) not the usurper (Antichrist). He rides the white horse of conquest, and His victory is sure. His greatness is in the spiritual qualities of His person: He is faithful, true, righteous. His eyes of fire penetrate our sinfulness and expose our spiritual inadequacy. His "many crowns" were probably received from the redeemed, who cast them at His feet in worship (Revelation 4:10). The fact that these crowns are "many" totally upstages the seven crowns of the dragon (Revelation 12:3) and the ten crowns of the beast (Revelation 13:1). His unknown name is a "secret" or "wonder" (see Judges 13:18; Isaiah 9:6). He is Jehovah God Himself—the *Yahweh* (YHVH) of the Old Testament. He is the I Am whose name is "above every name" (Philippians 2:9).

John wants us to know for certain who this is, so he calls Jesus by his favorite name: the Word (Greek, *logos*) of God (see John 1:1). Christ is the self-disclosure of the Almighty. He is the personal revelation of God to man. He is the personal Word who is also the author of the written word. The One revealed is the ultimate revelator of the revelation: Jesus the Christ.

When the Savior returns, He will come from heaven with His bride at His side. The church militant will be the church triumphant. Her days of conflict, rejection, and persecution will be over. She will return victorious with her Warrior-King-Husband.

Every true believer who reads the prediction of Christ's triumphal return in Revelation 19:11-16 should be overwhelmed by its significance. Think about it: We will be in that heavenly army with Him when He returns from glory. In fact, you might want to take a pen and circle the word "armies" in Revelation 19:14 and write your name in the margin next to the verse, for *you* will be there when He returns!

The destiny of the believer is now fully clarified. Our future hope includes 1) the rapture, 2) Christ's return, and 3) Christ's reign. The church must be raptured to heaven prior to the marriage and prior to her return from heaven with Christ. In the rapture, we will go up to heaven. In the return, we will come back to Earth. And in the millennium, we will reign with Christ on the Earth for 1000 years (Revelation 20:4).

## Lesson 9
# The Glorious Appearing

Are you weary from living in this world filled with injustice, pain, and sorrow? Do you tire of struggling with temptation, dealing with difficult people, and enduring society's incessant assaults on that which is godly or biblical? Have you experienced moments when you wish Jesus would hasten His return and make all things right?

We trust that is indeed the case with you...that you are among those who live in eager anticipation of the "glorious appearing of our great God and Savior Jesus Christ" (Titus 2:13). After all, as Christians, "our citizenship is in heaven," from which we should "eagerly wait for the Savior" (Philippians 3:20). We don't fit in this present world, and as our love for Christ grows, our affections for the world should correspondingly diminish.

The return of Christ will have two phases—the rapture, in which the church is taken up to heaven before the Tribulation, and the return, in which Christ and the church will descend victoriously upon the earth. That there are two phases is very evident when we observe that there are at least 15 differences in the descriptions of Christ's coming that cannot be reconciled into one event.

### The 15 Differences Between the Rapture and the Glorious Appearing

| Rapture/Blessed Hope | Glorious Appearing |
|---|---|
| 1. Christ comes in the air for His own | 1. Christ comes with His own to earth |
| 2. Rapture of all Christians | 2. No one raptured |
| 3. Christians taken to the Father's house | 3. Resurrected saints do not see Father's house |

| Rapture/Blessed Hope | Glorious Appearing |
|---|---|
| 4. No judgment on earth | 4. Christ judges inhabitants of earth |
| 5. Church taken to heaven | 5. Christ sets up His kingdom on earth |
| 6. Imminent—could happen any moment | 6. Cannot occur for at least 7 years |
| 7. No signs | 7. Many signs for Christ's physical coming |
| 8. For believers only | 8. Affects all humanity |
| 9. Time of joy | 9. Time of mourning |
| 10. Before the "day of wrath" (Tribulation) | 10. Immediately after Tribulation (Matthew 24) |
| 11. No mention of Satan | 11. Satan bound in abyss for 1000 years |
| 12. The judgment seat of Christ | 12. No time or place for judgment seat |
| 13. Marriage of the Lamb | 13. His bride descends with Him |
| 14. Only His own see Him | 14. Every eye will see Him |
| 15. Tribulation begins | 15. 1000-year kingdom of Christ begins |

1. Read Revelation 19:11-16, which provides the most glorious description of Christ's return in all the Bible. Who is the rider on the white horse, and what does He do (verse 11)?

2. How is this rider described in verse 12?

3. What name is given to this rider (verse 13)?

4. Who follows this rider (verse 14)? What additional light does 1 Thessalonians 3:13 and 4:14 shed on the identity of these followers?

5. What will this rider do, according to Revelation 19:15?

6. What special title is given to this rider in verse 16?

7. With whom will this rider do battle when He returns (verse 19)? What will be the outcome of this encounter (verses 20-21)?

## *Applying Prophecy to Everyday Life*

Are you looking forward to Christ returning to establish His rule on earth? Write two or three reasons you are especially excited about living in this future kingdom.

# 10

# THE BATTLE OF ARMAGEDDON

Many people believe we are living in the end times—an era during which the world will be plunged into a series of cataclysmic wars. By the time these wars end, perhaps as much as three-fourths of the earth's population will have died. "Armageddon theology" is the popular designation for Bible prophecies about the end of the world.

In the secular mind, such beliefs are little understood. Some people have even gone so far as to accuse evangelical Christians of trying to hasten the end by advocating a nuclear war as a divine instrument to punish the wicked and complete God's plan for history. These people seem to think that because Christians look forward to the second coming of Christ, they will try to hasten that event.

Yet no right-thinking person wants war, no matter what his views of the end times. We all sense the ominous finality of the predictions about the last days and pray that God will stay His hand of judgment. Only an ignorant person could think that humans are clever enough to avoid a final confrontation of disastrous consequences. We may dodge the apocalyptic bullet a few more times, but sooner or later, we will have to face the final moment of history.

## The Last Battle

Revelation 19 ends with the final triumph of Christ over the Antichrist, presumably at or after the Battle of Armageddon. The passage itself refers to the carnage as the "supper of the great God" (Revelation 19:17). While Armageddon is mentioned by name only in Revelation 16:16, it is mentioned two verses earlier in what is called the "battle of that great day of God Almighty" (Revelation 16:14). This includes the pouring of the seventh bowl (Revelation 16:17), the great earthquake (16:18-20), and the fall of Babylon (17:1–19:6).

Armageddon is the final battle of the Tribulation period. It will take place in Israel in conjunction with the second coming of Christ. The battle involves a series of conflicts in and around Jerusalem, as described in Daniel 11:40-45; Joel 3:9-17; Zechariah 14:1-3; and Revelation 16:14-16. It will occur in the final days of the Tribulation when the kings of the world are gathered together for the "battle of that great day of God" (Revelation 16:14).

The site of Armageddon is 50 miles north of Jerusalem in the Valley of Jezreel. This area is also known as the Plain of Esdraelon, near the ruins of the ancient city of Megiddo. The invading army is pictured moving toward Jerusalem from the north and east. The Old Testament prophets all identify Jerusalem as the site where the final phase of the battle will occur.

At Armageddon, the Antichrist, the kings of the earth, and their combined armies will be gathered against Christ and the church to make war. The term "gathered" (Greek, *sunagoge*) in Revelation 19:19 is the same word used in Revelation 16:16 in relation to Armageddon, which tells us both are talking about the same conflict. As we noted earlier, Armageddon may actually be a war of which this is the final battle. The carnage is so extensive that it includes kings, captains, mighty men, cavalry, small men, and great men (19:18).

The prophets predict that God will intervene in human history on behalf of His people and will destroy the Antichrist's army at Jerusalem. Zechariah predicts the battle will end when the Messiah touches down on the Mount of Olives, splits it in half, and enters Jerusalem triumphantly through the Eastern Gate.

## The Victorious Return

When Christ returns, He will come *with* His church, not to *spare* His church. He will return to spare the human race. He Himself predicted that "unless those days were shortened, no flesh would be saved" (Matthew 24:22). He will return in triumph and win the battle by the power of His spoken word ("the sword...from his mouth"—Revelation 19:21). He will speak, and the battle will be over! Just as He spoke, "Peace, be still!" and the storm ceased (Mark 4:39), so the greatest conflagration in human history will come to an end by His spoken word. He who spoke the worlds into existence will speak and the enemy will be slain. The battle will then be over, and Christ and His church will at last be victorious.

Revelation 19 ends with the Antichrist and the False Prophet defeated. Both will be cast alive into the Lake of Fire. This punishment dramatizes the seriousness of their offense and the finality of Christ's victory over them. The rest of the rebel army will be slain, but they will not be consigned to the Lake of Fire until the Great White Throne Judgment (Revelation 20:11-15). The fact that the Antichrist and the False Prophet are cast *alive* into the Lake of Fire, and that they are still there in Revelation 20:10, indicates that it is a place of eternal, conscious punishment.

In the meantime, Revelation 20:1-2 tells us that Satan will be bound in the bottomless pit for 1000 years before he, too, is cast into the Lake of Fire. In each case, it is Christ who sends them into the Lake of Fire, not Satan. Jesus alone will determine the final destiny of unbelievers, as well as of the unholy trinity.

As dramatic and climactic as this chapter is, it only sets the stage for the Millennium and the eternal state. The marriage of the Lamb began with the opening ceremonies in heaven. Now the King and His bride will rule for 1000 years on earth. During this time, all of God's promised blessings to Israel will be fulfilled literally as the devastated earth again blossoms like a rose.

## When Will This Happen?

The Old Testament prophets predicted that the Messiah will come to deliver Israel when the nations repent and turn to the one "whom they pierced" (Zechariah 12:10). In response to their prayers, Christ will return to deliver Israel from the clutches of the Antichrist. He will return bodily and literally, just as He departed in His ascension to heaven.

Every biblical text that deals with Christ's triumphant return emphasizes the great victory He will win at that time. For example, the apostle Paul wrote: "Then the lawless one will be revealed, whom the Lord will consume with the breath of His mouth and destroy with the brightness of His coming" (2 Thessalonians 2:8).

The Battle of Armageddon ends with Christ proclaiming victory over the Antichrist, the False Prophet, and the devil. Revelation 19:20 declares that the Antichrist and the False Prophet will both be captured and be "cast alive into the lake of fire." Revelation 20:2-3 adds that Satan will be bound in the abyss or bottomless pit for 1000 years. During this time, Satan will be inactive and thus unable to deceive the nations any longer.

So, the Battle of Armageddon will bring the Tribulation to an end and usher in 1000 years of peace and blessing through the reign of Christ on earth. It is during this time that all of God's prophetic promises to Israel will finally be fulfilled, and Christ will reign in peace on David's throne.

# Lesson 10
# **The Battle of Armageddon**

The word Armageddon has Hebrew roots, with the word *har* meaning "mountain" or "hill," and *Magedon* being a reference to the ruins of an ancient city that overlooks the Valley of Esdraelon in northern Israel. In the Battle of Armageddon, the leaders of the world, headed by Antichrist, will gather their armies to fight against the nation of Israel. Through the ages, Satan has longed to eradicate Israel because he wants to prevent God's promises from being fulfilled through His chosen people.

The Battle of Armageddon will be Satan's last attempt, and as always, he will not succeed. As 1 Kings 8:56 says, "There has not failed one word of all [God's] good promise." Up to today, God's track record for fulfilling His promises stands at 100 percent, and there is absolutely nothing Satan can do to change the outcome of the prophecies that have not yet been fulfilled.

1. Briefly describe the scene in Revelation 16:12. Why does this happen?

2. Whom do the spirits of demons gather together in Revelation 16:14?

3. Where does this gathering take place (verse 16)?

4. What scene does Zechariah 14:2-3 describe for us in Jerusalem?

5. What will the Lord do in response (verses 8-9)?

6. According to Zechariah 12:10 and Romans 11:26-27, what miracle will take place?

7. During the battle, where will Christ make His victorious descent (see Zechariah 14:4)?

8. How does Matthew 24:29-31 describe Christ's return? Who will witness this event?

### *Applying Prophecy to Everyday Life*

In the Battle of Armageddon, the Antichrist's forces will be so massive and daunting as to make it appear that the situation is hopeless. But when Jesus returns, Antichrist's defeat will be instant and complete. God is still in full control of all that happens; He who brought about the perfect fulfillment of every single one of the prophecies of Christ's first coming will also bring about the perfect fulfillment of every single one of the prophecies of Christ's second coming.

What level of comfort and encouragement does this give you, in light of the steadily worsening evil in our world?

# 11

# THE MILLENNIAL KINGDOM

Throughout the Old and New Testaments are numerous references to the kingdom of Christ, the long-anticipated time when the Lord Jesus Himself will reign upon the Earth. This is, in fact, one of the more frequently mentioned subjects in the Bible. Many names are used to describe this period including the kingdom age, the age of peace, the reign of Christ, and the Millennium. Not to be confused with the eternal realm of heaven, this temporary kingdom will be a time of peace on Earth, which mankind has always yearned for.

Throughout the centuries, every scheme devised by man to forge a utopian world has failed. Why? There are two reasons. First, man has a sinful and degenerate heart and cannot produce a world of peace, no matter how hard he tries. Second, as long as Satan is roaming free on the Earth, there will always be war. He is not only a deceiver, but a hater of men who continues to pit nations against each other. The proliferation of war even in this era of the United Nations is evidence that man will always fail in his attempts to secure peace. The United Nations was established to help bring about a permanent discontinuation of war. However, since its inception, there have been more wars and more bloodshed than in any comparable period of world history.

When Jesus taught His followers to pray in Matthew 6:10 "Thy kingdom come" (KJV), He was referring specifically to the millennial kingdom. It will certainly be the most incredible kingdom in all of human history—a kingdom in which Jesus, the anointed King, will have the nations for His inheritance (Psalm 2:8), when "the wolf also shall dwell with the lamb" (Isaiah 11:6), and "the earth shall be full of the knowledge of the LORD" (Isaiah 11:9).

Just how long will this kingdom last? There is only one chapter in the Bible that reveals this information, and that is Revelation 20. There, we find the phrase "thousand years" mentioned six times in the first seven verses. More specifically, verse 6 says, "Blessed and holy is he who has part in the first resurrection. Over such the second death has no power, but they shall be priests of God and of Christ, and shall reign with Him a thousand years."

## Understanding the Millennium

The word *millennium* is a Latin term that means "a thousand years." Despite the many biblical references to the millennial reign of Christ, and despite the fact that Christians will play a vital role in it, most believers know very little about this critical period in our planet's future. Before we find out more about this kingdom, let's first examine the three major views people have held historically regarding the millennial kingdom.

*Premillennialism* is the belief that the second coming of Christ to set up His earthly kingdom will occur prior to the millennial age. This is the view accepted by nearly all Bible scholars who take the Scriptures literally and at face value whenever possible.

There are others who believe the world is going to become more and more "Christianized" in time and, as a result, usher in the kingdom of Christ on its own merits. In this scenario, Jesus would return at the end of the Millennium to an already-righteous earth. This belief is known as *postmillennialism.* A third viewpoint, known as *amillennialism,* holds to a nonliteral or spiritualized interpretation of Scripture and attempts to allegorically explain away the coming Millennium. In the amillennial scheme, there is no anticipation of a literal reign of Christ on earth.

The early Christians were unquestionably premillennialists. In fact, the disciples and those whom they taught anticipated the return of Christ and the establishment of His kingdom on Earth in their lifetime. There are detractors of the premillennial view who claim that it is a relatively new theory, but the truth is that premillennialism was the dominant view held during the first three centuries of the early church.

Premillennilists believe that the rapture, the Tribulation, and the glorious appearing of Christ will all occur before the beginning of the Millennium. During this time, Satan will be bound for 1000 years and a theocratic kingdom of peace on earth will ensue, with Jesus as its King. According to Revelation chapter 20, the righteous will have already been raised from the dead prior to the Millennium (at the time of the rapture) and will participate with Christ in the reign of His kingdom.

## Confusion About the Millennium

Toward the end of the third century A.D., the allegorizing of Scripture began to consume theological ideology. Philosophy replaced the study of Scripture, and premillennialism, along with many other important biblical teachings (such as salvation by grace), fell into disrepute. Not until after the Reformation of the sixteenth century was there a revival of premillennial thought. As the twentieth century began to unfold, Bible institutes and Christian colleges across America sprang up emphasizing a solid, literal interpretation of the Bible, and with them, a return to premillennialism. Today, despite continued attacks, premillennialism remains the most dominant perspective of the three millennial views.

Amillennialism holds that there will be no literal kingdom on the Earth following the second coming of Christ. It tends to spiritualize and allegorize all prophecies concerning the Millennium, and yet-to-be-fulfilled prophecies relating to Israel are attributed to the church instead. Amillennialists also believe Satan was bound during Christ's first appearance on earth 2000 years ago, an argument that can hardly be substantiated when one considers the present condition of our world and Peter's observation that "the devil walks about like a roaring lion" (1 Peter 5:8).

Furthermore, amillennialists aren't sure whether the Millennium is being fulfilled currently on earth or whether it's being fulfilled by the saints in heaven. However, they tend to agree that our current state of affairs is probably as good as the world is going to get and that the eternal realm, not the millennial kingdom, will immediately follow the second coming of Christ. Those who hold to this view go to great lengths to avoid the simple and plain literal interpretation of Scripture regarding the binding of Satan and the reign of Christ for one thousand years on earth (Revelation 20:2-7).

Postmillennialism is the belief that the world will continue to get better and better until the entire world is christianized, at which time Christ will return to a kingdom already flourishing in peace. Although this view was popular at the beginning of the twentieth century, it has all but died out as a result of the World Wars, the Great Depression, and the overwhelming escalation of moral evil in our society. However, those of the *preterist* persuasion are making a concerted attempt to resuscitate the postmillennial theory but are not gaining much headway, primarily because most lay people who read the Bible tend to take it literally. And if one takes Bible prophecy literally, it becomes apparent that the world will continue to get worse, not better, prior to the Millennium.

## The Premillennial Hope

According to the premillennial view, the rapture of the church, followed by the Tribulation and the glorious appearing of Jesus, will take place prior to Christ's establishment of His 1000-year kingdom. As the prophet Isaiah predicted:

> Unto us a Child is born, unto us a Son is given; and the government will be upon His shoulder. And His name will be called Wonderful, Counselor, Mighty God, Everlasting

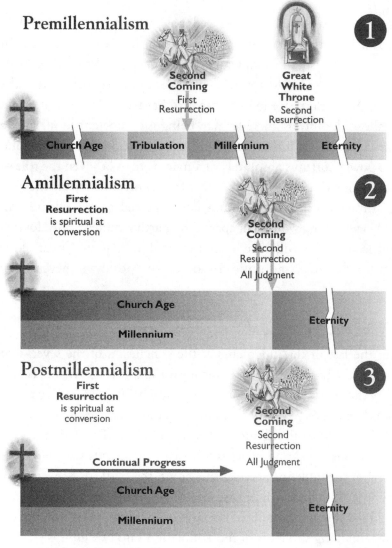

Excerpted and adapted from Tim LaHaye and Thomas Ice, *Charting the End Times* (Eugene, OR: Harvest House Publishers, 2001), p. 129.

Father, Prince of Peace. Of the increase of His government and peace there will be no end (Isaiah 9:6).

Although the first part of this prophecy was fulfilled during Christ's first appearance on Earth, the second part has yet to be fulfilled. At no time was the government on Jesus' shoulder when He was here 2000 years ago, nor has there ever been a global government of peace. This kingdom will occur when our Lord returns to the Earth at His second coming and establishes His millennial reign on Earth (Revelation 5:10).

Many of the one-world government advocates today believe that the only hope for world peace in our time is to have a world dictator. From a biblical standpoint, no mere human being is competent to fill such a position. History has proven time and again that power corrupts and absolute power corrupts absolutely. If a man were to be given the role of world dictator (which will, in fact, occur for a short time during the horrifying Tribulation period that immediately precedes the Millennium), inevitably everything would fall apart. The Earth requires a holy, loving, merciful leader who will treat mankind equitably. Jesus Christ alone qualifies for that role, and until He comes, the world will never know true peace.

## How Will the Millennial Kingdom Begin?

After the last of the judgments at the conclusion of the seven-year Tribulation, the Lord will appear in the sky for all to see. He will be accompanied by the angels and by His bride, the church. "Behold, He is coming with clouds, and every eye will see Him, even they who pierced Him. And all the tribes of the earth will mourn because of Him" (Revelation 1:7).

The glorious appearing of Jesus Christ in the clouds will signal the beginning of the millennial era. At this point, the Battle of Armageddon will end, the Antichrist will be cast into the Lake of Fire, and Satan will be bound for the duration of the 1000-year kingdom. Jesus will also divide the remaining survivors of the Tribulation into two groups:

> When the Son of Man comes in His glory, and all the holy angels with Him, then He will sit on the throne of His glory. All the nations will be gathered before Him, and He will separate them one from another, as a shepherd divides his sheep from the goats. And He will set the sheep on His right hand, but the goats on the left. Then the King will say to those on His right hand, "Come, you blessed of My Father, inherit the

kingdom prepared for you from the foundation of the world"
(Matthew 25:31-34).

The "goats" mentioned here are the millions of unsaved and unbe-
lieving followers of the Antichrist who will take the mark of the beast,
persecute the Jews, and kill the Christians during the Tribulation. They
will immediately be cast into hell. The "sheep" are those Gentile individuals who refused to take the mark and befriended and protected the
Jews during this period. It is these surviving Jews and Gentiles who will
enter the millennial kingdom in their natural bodies and repopulate the
earth during the 1000 years of Christ's rule.

The other group of people who will occupy the earth during the
Millennium will be those with immortal, resurrected bodies. This would
include everyone who received a new body at the time of the rapture
and the Tribulation saints who are to be resurrected at the appearance
of Christ. It is quite probable that it will also include Gentile believers
whom Jesus said would "sit down with Abraham, Isaac, and Jacob in the
kingdom" (Matthew 8:11). This group will not procreate, but will rule
and reign with Christ during this period of time. Only those who exist
in their natural bodies will continue to have the ability to procreate.

During the Millennium, Jesus, the Holy Judge, will reign supreme.
His kingdom will be one of righteousness. Since Satan is bound for
the duration, there will be no deception (although at the end of the
Millennium, Satan will be briefly released before being bound for eternity). This era will be a time of global peace without any fear of fellow
man. It will also be a time of longevity. People's lifespans will increase
dramatically; consequently, the Earth's population could reach unprecedented numbers, most of whom will be believers in Christ.

One of the characteristics of our present time is that so few people
really know about God and the Bible. But during the Millennium, it
won't be necessary to preach the gospel anymore because those who
dwell on the earth will instinctively know it:

> I will put My law in their minds, and write it on their hearts;
> and I will be their God, and they shall be My people. No

more shall every man teach his neighbor, and every man his brother, saying, "Know the LORD," for they all shall know Me, from the least of them to the greatest of them, says the LORD. For I will forgive their iniquity, and their sin I will remember no more (Jeremiah 31:33-34).

Everyone should realize that the coming 1000-year kingdom will be the most incredible era ever in Earth's history. It will be a time of unprecedented peace, when those who have accepted Jesus Christ as their Lord and Savior will be able to rule and reign along with their loving King. It will most certainly be a time best described by the word *utopia*. For in that day,

they shall beat their swords into plowshares, and their spears into pruning hooks; nation shall not lift up sword against nation, neither shall they learn war anymore (Isaiah 2:4).

Such world peace is beyond finite human comprehension. There is no way depraved humanity will ever be able to bring about such conditions on Earth. But, thank God, such will be reality when Jesus returns to reign on the Earth.

# The Millennial Kingdom

After the Tribulation, the Lord Jesus Christ will reign on the Earth for 1000 years…after which He will then usher us into eternity. During this 1000-year kingdom, humanity will get a taste of what it's like to live under God's rule rather than man's. From the time of the fall, people have tried time and again to bring about an existence marked by true and lasting peace, but no one has succeeded. No matter how hard we try, we are destined for failure because we are all fallen creatures.

In the millennial kingdom, however, we will know perfect justice and peace. Society will not be directed by the fickle whims of men, but by our all-knowing and ever-faithful Savior. We will literally experience heaven on Earth!

1. On pages 98-99, three different views of the millennial kingdom are presented. Name each view, and describe it in a sentence or two.

   –

   –

   –

2. Revelation 20:1-6 provides for us some details about the millennial kingdom. Who will be bound at the beginning of Christ's 1000-year reign, where will he be bound, and for how long (verses 1-3)?

3. Briefly describe how the world will be a different place on account of the fact Satan is bound (see Isaiah 2:4 and Jeremiah 31:33-34).

4. Read Revelation 20:4, then Revelation 6:9-11. Who will be among those who reign with Christ during the millennial kingdom?

5.  Revelation 20:6 mentions the "first resurrection," that is, the people who populate the millennial kingdom. According to 1 Corinthians 15:23 and 1 Thessalonians 4:13-18, who will be among those in the first resurrection?

6.  What will happen at the end of the millennial kingdom, according to Revelation 20:7-10?

7.  Where will Satan, the Antichrist, and False Prophet receive their punishment (see Revelation 20:10)? For how long?

## *Applying Prophecy to Everyday Life*

While Christ's rule on Earth is still a future event, if you're a Christian, He lives and rules in your heart right now. Are you living in a way that acknowledges His kingship? In what ways can you grow more in this area?

## 12
# THE GREAT WHITE THRONE JUDGMENT

One of the most sobering passages in the Bible is Revelation 20:11-15. Here, unbelievers are given a glimpse of what their eventual encounter with God will be like. This passage describes the Great White Throne Judgment. This fearsome event will occur at the end of Christ's 1000-year reign. In fact, it is the last event scheduled before we enter the age of the new heaven and new earth as outlined in Revelation chapters 21 and 22.

The great statesman Daniel Webster was once asked, "What is the greatest thought that has ever passed through your mind?" Webster instantly replied, "My accountability to God." Nowhere is man's accountability to his Creator more clearly defined than in this particular section of Scripture:

> I saw a great white throne and Him who sat on it, from whose face the earth and the heaven fled away. And there was found no place for them. And I saw the dead, small and great, standing before God, and books were opened. And another book was opened, which is the Book of Life. And the dead

were judged according to their works, by the things which were written in the books. The sea gave up the dead who were in it, and Death and Hades delivered up the dead who were in them. And they were judged, each one according to his works. Then Death and Hades were cast into the lake of fire. This is the second death. And anyone not found written in the Book of Life was cast into the lake of fire (Revelation 20:11-15).

The Bible makes it abundantly clear in a number of passages that judgment for all people will most certainly follow death. For example, Hebrews 9:27 says, "It is appointed for men to die once, but after this the judgment" (Hebrews 9:27). Not only does Hebrews 9:27 dispute the pagan concept of reincarnation, it also suggests that everyone will eventually be judged. Unfortunately, most people try not to think about that while they are alive. And the criteria by which we are judged will be determined by our status in Christ. Believers and unbelievers will be judged at different times and in very different ways.

## The People Who Will Be Judged
### Judgment of Believers

Immediately following the rapture, believers will stand before the judgment seat of Christ in heaven as described in 2 Corinthians 5:10. Here, the resurrected saints will receive rewards for the good works that they performed while on Earth. Bad works as well as good works performed with wrong motives will be "burned," as revealed in 1 Corinthians 3:11-15:

No other foundation can anyone lay than that which is laid, which is Jesus Christ. Now if anyone builds on this foundation with gold, silver, precious stones, wood, hay, straw, each one's work will become clear; for the Day will declare it, because it will be revealed by fire; and the fire will test each one's work, of what sort it is. If anyone's work which he has built on it endures, he will receive a reward. If anyone's work is burned, he will suffer loss; but he himself will be saved, yet so as through fire.

Note that at no time is any believer's salvation in jeopardy. Simple faith in Jesus Christ guarantees a believer's place in heaven. His good works, however, will determine his *status* in heaven. Appearing before the judgment seat of Christ will be a time of indescribable joy for those who faithfully served Jesus Christ while on Earth.

## Judgment of Unbelievers

That is a far cry from what will happen to the unbelievers sentenced to appear before the Great White Throne at the end of the Millennium. No believer in Jesus will be judged at the Great White Throne Judgment—only unbelievers. Revelation 20:12 describes them as the "dead, small and great." These people, regardless of their stature or position, died without acknowledging and accepting Jesus Christ's payment for their sins. Whether in the earth or sea, or in a grave or mausoleum, the ashes or remains of these deceased will one day be raised and united with their souls so that they can stand in a resurrected form before the Great White Throne.

During this judgment, various books will be opened that contain the records of every deed and thought (including those performed in secret) of every unbeliever: "God will bring every work into judgment, including every hidden thing, whether good or evil" (Ecclesiastes 12:14).

Apparently God has prepared a complete set of books that reveal everything about a person's life. These books will be opened on judgment day. It's a little unnerving to think that each of us may have a recording angel following us around, tabulating our every word or deed. The actions and intentions of those who have foolishly chosen not to have their sins erased by the sacrifice of Jesus will be judged according to the law of the Old Testament. As Galatians 3:10 reveals, those who live under the law, and not under Christ, will be judged by the law. Unless we accept God's mercy in the form of His Son, we cannot be found righteous, "for all have sinned and fall short of the glory of God" (Romans 3:23).

## The Criteria of Judgment

Hebrews 2:2 tells us that "every transgression and disobedience receive[s] a just reward." This is consistent with the justice of God and seems to indicate that there will be different levels of punishment in hell. A relatively moral citizen such as a doctor, teacher, or nice old neighbor who has lived a comparatively good life (though short of the standard of God) would not be subjected to the same punishment as someone such as Adolph Hitler, whose regime murdered millions of God's chosen people. Likewise, those heathen who never heard the gospel will be judged accordingly and certainly far less severe than those who heard His message repeatedly and rejected it. Matthew 11:21-24 reinforces this idea. In this passage of Scripture, Jesus explains that the people who heard His message and rejected it would be subjected to greater condemnation than the sinners who lived in the cities of Sodom and Gomorrah.

The Great White Throne Judgment is for unbelievers, who will be judged by the standards of God's law. During this judgment, the Book of Life will be opened just to make sure of a person's eternal status. If a person's name does not appear, he or she will be cast into the Lake of Fire for all eternity. This checking of the Book of Life serves to highlight God's mercy. No one will be unjustly condemned. Second Peter 3:9 states that "The Lord is...not willing that any should perish but that all should come to repentance." When Jesus died on the cross, He took upon Himself the sins of every person both past and future. God desires that all accept His gift of salvation but, unfortunately, multitudes through the ages have chosen instead to ignore this free gift and consequently have lost their opportunity for eternal life with Him.

Revelation 3:5 indicates believers can never be blotted out from the Book of Life. Revelation 21:27 tells us that the only people who will enter the Holy City (heaven) are "those who are written in the Lamb's Book of Life." It is therefore essential that one have his or her name written in this book if he or she wants to go to heaven.

## The Identity of the Judge

Who is the Judge that will be sitting on the Great White Throne? Acts 17:31 indicates it is the One who was raised "from the dead." John 5:22 tells us, "The Father judges no one, but has committed all judgment to the Son." Thus, it is Jesus Christ Himself who will sit on the Great White Throne. As Hebrews 4:13 says, "All things are naked and open to the eyes of Him to whom we must give account." It will be a sobering day indeed for those who find themselves standing before the very Judge whom they have mocked, rejected, ignored, or cursed. On that day, all will wish they had accepted His free gift of salvation, but by then it will be too late to do so.

People who have elected to ignore the countless advantages of having a relationship with Christ, including His free gift of eternal life, often provide well-worn excuses in order to somehow validate their neglect of spiritual matters. One such excuse can be phrased like this: "I'm not interested in learning about a God who demonstrates His cruelty by sending people to hell." Of course, such a statement can only be based on a lack of knowledge. As Scripture clearly indicates, our God is a merciful God who has gone to tremendous lengths in order to rescue His creation.

In a sense, those who end up in hell will go there because ultimately they prefer it to the alternative of spending eternity in heaven. Such a statement might surprise you, but consider this: What was the first thing Adam and Eve did when they sinned? They tried to hide from their all-knowing Creator. Why? Because once they had sinned, they couldn't stand to be in His Holy presence.

Those who accept Jesus' payment for their sins at some point during their life will be free from the penalty of their sins and, upon entering heaven in their new body, will be able to fellowship with their Creator. By contrast, those who refuse to accept Jesus as their Lord and Savior will still "posess" their sins when they die. Theoretically, then, they would feel extremely uncomfortable in heaven, to put it mildly. They would feel the same way Adam and Eve felt in God's presence after they fell.

## An Abundance of Warnings

One reason God has given us so much information in His Word about the judgment that awaits those who reject or neglect Him is because He doesn't want anyone to face eternity in hell. His desire is for everyone to choose salvation and thereby live with Him forever in heaven. Jesus Himself warned, "Most assuredly, I say to you, unless one is born again, he cannot see the kingdom of God" (John 3:3).

Unless a person is born again (born anew from above) and has their sins erased, he or she will not be prepared for the spiritual delights of heaven. What's more, heaven cannot be contaminated by sin. Heaven would cease to be heaven if sin were to enter into it. A Christian is fit for heaven not because he is good or because he deserves it, but because he chose to accept God's pardon for his sins and the cleansing power of Christ's death on the cross. And those who do not make this choice will not be fit for heaven.

During this life, we are all confronted with a choice. We can admit we are sinners in need of a Savior and invite Jesus into our lives, or we can reject Him. Where we spend eternity will be determined by that choice. If you have not made a decision for Christ, please do so before it's too late.

# The Great White Throne Judgment

Christians can look forward to the future with great anticipation because they have the promise of heaven. But not unbelievers. For them, the future is one big unknown. And the warning that they will one day face judgment brings great trepidation to their hearts.

Unfortunately, there's a common misperception that everyone will be judged at one time—both Christians and unbelievers. But in actuality, God's children will face a judgment related not to their salvation, but to rewards based on their works on Earth. And unbelievers will face the Great White Throne Judgment, which is the final judgment for all people of all ages who rejected God during their time here on Earth.

So that we might better distinguish between the two judgments, let's look at them more carefully.

## *The Judgment of Christians*

1. Read 1 Corinthians 3:10-15. Who is the foundation upon which Christians build (verses 10-11)?

2. What different kinds of building material will Christians use (verse 12)?

3. What will the fire in verse 13 be used for?

4. What will happen if a person's work endures? If his or her works don't endure?

## *The Judgment of Unbelievers*

1. Read Revelation 20:11-15. What scene is described in verse 12?

2. Will anyone be able to escape this judgment (see verse 13)?

3. What are these people judged according to (see verses 12b and 13b)?

4. What will happen to those whose names are not found in the Book of Life (verse 15)?

5. What can we learn from Matthew 25:41 and Mark 9:33-34 about the Lake of Fire?

6. How long will this punishment last (see Matthew 25:41,46)?

7. What does Luke 16:26 say about those who are in heaven or hell?

## *Applying Prophecy to Everyday Life*

As Hebrews 9:27 says, "It is appointed for men to die once, but after this the judgment." In other words, there is no second chance. Are you certain about your eternal destination? If not, see pages 121-22 of this workbook and read about what it means to trust Christ as your personal Savior. And if you are a Christian, we trust that the sober reality of future judgment burdens your heart to share the good news of Jesus Christ with friends and family members who are unbelievers.

# 13
# HEAVEN AND ETERNAL LIFE

The concept of life after death is not unique to Christianity and is, in fact, the universal dream of mankind. It is so integrated into the human psyche that nearly every religion has been built upon this expectation. While opinions, philosophies, and religions may differ, very few people consider death to be the end of life. From the primitive tribesmen of the jungles to the sophisticated mystics of the East, virtually every tradition has some system of belief regarding the afterlife. Even some of those who have attempted suicide have confessed that their ultimate rationale was to find themselves, hopefully, in a better set of circumstances in the next life.

Why do most people hold to this belief in life after death? Could it be intuitive? Did God place this thought within us? If so, we expect the Bible to reveal truthful insights about it. Indeed, Christianity tells without a doubt the most beautiful story of the afterlife—for believers. The Bible provides far more believable details about the next life than any other so-called "holy" book. That should come as no surprise to Christians, who believe the source of the Bible to be the Creator Himself.

Christianity is built on the foundation of the resurrection of Jesus

Christ. The Lord provided His own resurrection as the paramount sign of His deity. Although Jesus' disciples were a defeated group following His crucifixion, they were subsequently motivated to world evangelism following His resurrection. As Luke documented in the first chapter of Acts, "He...presented Himself alive after His suffering by many infallible proofs." Thus, the Christian belief in life after death is based upon the fact of Christ's resurrection.

## The Promise of Eternal Life

Jesus promised His followers, "Because I live, you shall live also." Not surprisingly, no one in the Bible speaks more about the resurrection than Jesus Christ Himself. In John 11:25-26, for example, He said, "I am the resurrection and the life. He who believes in Me, though he may die, he shall live. And whoever lives and believes in Me shall never die." Jesus was saying that although those who believe in Him may die physically, the real person, which is the soul and spirit, will never die. In John 5:24-29 Christ taught,

> Most assuredly, I say to you, he who hears My word and believes in Him who sent Me has everlasting life, and shall not come into judgment, but has passed from death into life. Most assuredly, I say to you, the hour is coming, and now is, when the dead will hear the voice of the Son of God; and those who hear will live. For as the Father has life in Himself, so He has granted the Son to have life in Himself, and has given Him authority to execute judgment also, because He is the Son of Man. Do not marvel at this; for the hour is coming in which all who are in the graves will hear His voice and come forth—those who have done good, to the resurrection of life, and those who have done evil, to the resurrection of condemnation.

From the above passage, we know that both the righteous and unrighteous will be resurrected. Eternal life is therefore guaranteed for all.

However, *where* and *how* that future will play out depends entirely on one's position in Christ.

## Our Eternal Destiny

Prior to the death, burial, and resurrection of Jesus Christ, all people who died were taken to a place known as *Sheol* or *Hades*. Speculated to be located at the center of the earth, this place had two compartments separated by a large chasm or gulf. The first section was known as "paradise" or the "place of comfort." This is where the Old Testament saints would go following death. On the other side of the great gulf was the "place of torment," where those who died without faith were held (see Luke 16:26). Ever since Jesus' resurrection, believers have not gone to the "place of comfort" in Sheol, but rather, have been instantly transported to heaven to be with the Lord (see 2 Corinthians 5:8). Unbelievers, on the other hand, are still taken to the "place of torment" in Sheol/Hades.

The word "heaven" appears nearly 600 times in the Bible. It can refer to three different places: 1) the atmospheric heaven or sky; 2) the planetary heaven where the sun, moon, and stars reside; or 3) the third heaven, which Paul speaks of in 2 Corinthians 12, where God dwells with His angels and His people. This is where believers who have died are today. Everything that is truly precious to us as Christians will be in this third heaven, including the triune God, our loved ones who are believers, our inheritance, our citizenship, and our eternal rewards. In other words, everything of eternal value will be there.

When the rapture occurs, we who are believers will instantly receive our new, immortal, resurrected bodies. At the rapture, Christ will come to take us home to the Father's house in heaven (John 14:1-4). Many of us look forward to that glorious day when we will see the unfathomable magnificence of heaven, be reunited with loved ones, and come face to face with Jesus, our Savior. What some of us fail to realize, however, is that immediately following the rapture, we will stand before the judgment seat of Christ and receive rewards, if any, for the good works we performed in the name of Christ during our time on Earth. Then, while

# The Eternal State

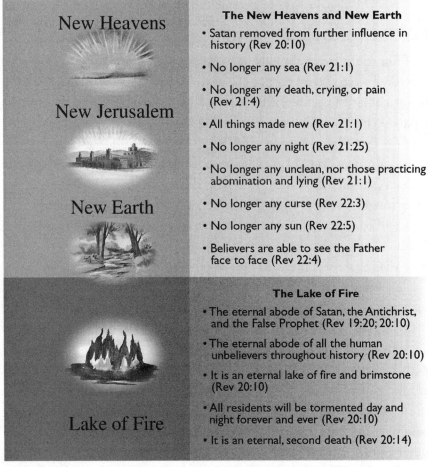

**The New Heavens and New Earth**

- Satan removed from further influence in history (Rev 20:10)

- No longer any sea (Rev 21:1)

- No longer any death, crying, or pain (Rev 21:4)

- All things made new (Rev 21:1)

- No longer any night (Rev 21:25)

- No longer any unclean, nor those practicing abomination and lying (Rev 21:1)

- No longer any curse (Rev 22:3)

- No longer any sun (Rev 22:5)

- Believers are able to see the Father face to face (Rev 22:4)

**The Lake of Fire**

- The eternal abode of Satan, the Antichrist, and the False Prophet (Rev 19:20; 20:10)

- The eternal abode of all the human unbelievers throughout history (Rev 20:10)

- It is an eternal lake of fire and brimstone (Rev 20:10)

- All residents will be tormented day and night forever and ever (Rev 20:10)

- It is an eternal, second death (Rev 20:14)

Excerpted and adapted from Tim LaHaye and Thomas Ice, *Charting the End Times* (Eugene, OR: Harvest House Publishers, 2001), p. 76.

still in heaven, we will participate in the Marriage of the Lamb, where we will become the bride of Christ (Revelation 19:7-9). Finally, at the conclusion of the Tribulation (which will take place while we believers are in heaven), we will return with Jesus to Earth and rule with Him during the 1000-year kingdom (Revelation 20:1-3).

The bodies of those who happen to be alive on Earth at the time of the rapture, along with the bodies of believers who have already died, will be changed from corruptible into incorruptible (see 1 Corinthians 15:52-54).

Presently, our bodies are unfit for heaven and must be transformed into bodies similar to Christ's resurrection body. These new, resurrected bodies (made from the elements of our old bodies gathered together by the Lord) will be recognizable, able to communicate, and able to eat, just as Jesus ate with His disciples after His resurrection (see Luke 24:41-43; John 21:9-14). Jesus demonstrated that He could walk through walls and travel great distances at the speed of thought in His resurrected body. Likewise, we will be able to do the same. In this new, sinless, immortal body, we will rule and reign with Christ throughout the Millennium, and afterward enter into the new heaven for all eternity.

## Eternal Punishment of the Lost

Contrasting sharply with the glorious future that awaits each and every believer, the fate of the unbeliever is simply too horrifying to even imagine. As mentioned earlier, at the moment of death, the unbeliever is instantly taken to the place of torment in hell (Greek, *hades*). According to Revelation 20:11-15, at the conclusion of the millennial kingdom, unbelievers will be resurrected and brought out of Sheol/Hades to stand before Jesus Christ at the Great White Throne Judgment. There, they will be judged "according to their works" (verse 13) using the Law of the Old Testament. Since none have been born again, and since their names do not appear in the Book of Life, none will be able to enter the kingdom of God. All these unbelievers will then be cast into the Lake of Fire, where they will be tormented for all eternity. Had they accepted Christ's free gift of salvation while they were alive on earth, they would not have had to be punished with eternal separation from God.

The term "lake of fire" appears five times in Revelation (19:20; 20:10,14,15; 21:8). It is a place of conscious punishment. At present, no one is in the Lake of Fire. Its first occupants will be the Beast and the False Prophet (Revelation 19:20). When unbelievers die today, they go immediately to hell (*hades*) to await their final trial at the Great White Throne Judgment. After that they will be condemned to the Lake of Fire for all eternity. Those cast into the Lake of Fire will experience what is called the "second death" (Revelation 21:8). The first death is physical death, whereas the second involves eternal punishment.

Hell is certainly a place of torment and punishment. But it serves only as a holding place for those awaiting trial. By contrast, the Lake of Fire is a place of permanent incarceration from which there is no release. In the New Testament, this place serves as a symbol of eternal punishment (see Matthew 25:41-46; Mark 9:44-48).

## New Heaven and New Earth

At the conclusion of Christ's 1000-year millennial reign on earth and the Great White Throne Judgment, the Bible describes the formation of "a new heaven and a new earth" (Revelation 21:1), of which the New Jerusalem, a city of indescribable beauty, will be the capitol. That there will be a major overhaul of the universe appears to have been part of God's plan all along, for it was promised through the Old Testament prophets:

> Behold, I create new heavens and a new earth; and the former shall not be remembered or come to mind. But be glad and rejoice forever in what I create; for behold, I create Jerusalem as a rejoicing, and her people a joy. I will rejoice in Jerusalem, and joy in My people; the voice of weeping shall no longer be heard in her, nor the voice of crying (Isaiah 65:17-19).

The last two chapters of the Bible describe the New Jerusalem in some detail, a magnificent eternal dwelling place for God and His people:

> Now I saw a new heaven and a new earth, for the first heaven and the first earth had passed away. Also there was no more sea. Then I, John, saw the holy city, New Jerusalem, coming down out of heaven from God, prepared as a bride adorned for her husband. And I heard a loud voice from heaven saying, "Behold, the tabernacle of God is with men, and He will dwell with them, and they shall be His people. God Himself will be with them and be their God. And God will wipe away every tear from their eyes; there shall be no more death, nor sorrow,

nor crying. There shall be no more pain, for the former things have passed away" (Revelation 21:1-4).

John goes on to describe the scene in heaven. The New Jerusalem is the abode of the saved of all time: Old Testament saints, New Testament believers, and the Tribulation and millennial saints alike. The entire redeemed family of God will live together there for all eternity. The gates are named for the 12 tribes of Israel, and the jeweled foundations for the 12 apostles (21:12-14). There will be no Temple in the New Jerusalem because God Almighty is there. And there will be no sun because the glory of God will fill the Eternal City.

In essence, the Eternal City will be "paradise regained." The river of life and the tree of life will be there (22:1-2). The curse of the law will be eradicated by the blood of the Lamb, and we will reign with Christ "forever and ever" (22:5). It is no wonder that the hope of heaven has always been the longing of every true believer.

## You Must Decide

Keep in mind that all of us are sinners from birth. The only reason some people will spend eternity in heaven is because they accepted Christ's payment for their sins while they were alive on the Earth. Those who end up in hell for all eternity will do so because they died without receiving Jesus as their Savior. Jesus Himself gave us clear directions on how to obtain admittance into heaven when He said, "I am the way, and the truth, and the life. No one comes to the Father except through Me" (John 14:6).

Only through Jesus Christ can we gain access to the Father who is in heaven. Romans 3:23 says all men have sinned, and Romans 6:23 says "the wages of sin is death." Only through faith in the Lord Jesus Christ and His work on the cross can we escape. There is no other way, and no second chance. "As many as received Him, to them He gave the right to become children of God, to those who believe in His name" (John 1:12).

Have you put your faith in Jesus Christ for what He did for you on the cross? Until you say yes, you can have no hope of spending eternity in heaven. You won't get there by doing the best you can. That will never be good enough. You can only get to heaven by believing that Jesus alone paid for your sins. He and He alone is good enough to get you to heaven. He did everything necessary to secure your salvation when He died for your sins on the cross. And it's up to you to decide whether or not He meant what He said when He promised, "He who believes in the Son has everlasting life" (John 3:36) and, "The one who comes to Me I will by no means cast out" (John 6:37).

In the Bible, God invites you to trust Jesus Christ as your personal Savior. Scripture says, "If you confess with your mouth the Lord Jesus and believe in your heart that God has raised him from the dead, you will be saved....For whoever calls on the name of the Lord shall be saved" (Romans 10:9,13). If you have not done this yet, why not call upon Him right now? Express your faith and trust in Him by praying something like this:

> *God, I know I have sinned against You and that I need Your forgiveness. I do believe with all my heart that Jesus died on the cross for my sins and that He rose from the dead, conquering sin. I am trusting Jesus and Him alone to forgive my sins, save my soul, and give me eternal life. Right now I take Him as my personal Savior and place all my faith and trust in Him. Praying this in Jesus' name, amen.*

# Heaven and Eternal Life

In the last two chapters of the Bible, God pulls back the curtain and gives us a glimpse of heaven. And what an incredible scene we see! The description of our future home is rich with details, and yet this is just a tiny preview of what's to come. Mere words are inadequate to describe what God has prepared for us in eternity.

1. In heaven, with whom will we dwell, according to Revelation 21:3?

2. What "former things" will have passed away (verse 4)?

3. What is the extent of our inheritance (verse 7)?

4. What will the New Jerusalem be made out of (verse 18)?

5. What does verse 23 tell us about our future home?

6. What will never enter this city (verse 27)?

7. To what tree will we have access once again (Revelation 22:2)?

8. What will be our occupation, according to Revelation 22:3?

9. How long will we reign alongside God (verse 5)?

## *Applying Prophecy to Everyday Living*

What do you look forward to most about heaven? How can you allow that to positively impact the way you are living today on Earth?

# A FINAL WORD:
## UNTIL HE COMES

The timing of the last days is in God's hands. From a human standpoint, it appears that we are standing on the threshold of the final frontier. The pieces of the puzzle are all in place. As the sands of time slip through the hourglass of eternity, we are all moving closer to an appointment with destiny. The question we all should be asking is, How much time is left?

The tension between dealing with today and anticipating tomorrow is one of the difficult realities of living the Christian life. We often find ourselves caught between the here and now and the hereafter. On the one hand, we need to be ready for Jesus to come at any moment. On the other hand, we have God-given responsibilities to fulfill in this world right now.

We are living in a time of great crisis, but it is also a time of great opportunity. We must be prepared for the challenges that lie ahead of us. New technologies will make our lives more convenient, but they will also make us more dependent on those conveniences. Medical advancements will continue to pose enormous challenges in the area of bioethics. The shifting sands of sociopolitical change will also challenge our national and international policies in the days ahead. We will find ourselves living in a very different world from the one into which we were born. All of these changes and challenges will confront us in the days ahead.

Preparing for Christ's return is something each one of us must do for ourselves. No one else can get our hearts ready to meet God. That's our own responsibility. Jesus urges us to do three things in view of His second coming:

1. Keep watching (Matthew 24:42).
2. Be ready (Matthew 24:44).
3. Keep serving (Matthew 24:46).

Jesus gave the Great Commission, telling the disciples they would be empowered by the Holy Spirit to be His witnesses in Jerusalem, Judea, Samaria, and "to the end of the earth" (Acts 1:8). Then, to their amazement, He ascended into heaven, leaving them gazing intently into the sky. Two men in white (probably angels) appeared and asked, "Why do you stand gazing up into heaven? This same Jesus, who was taken up from you into heaven, will so come in like manner as you saw Him go into heaven" (Acts 1:11).

All too often, today's Christians are just like those early disciples. We spend more time gazing into the sky and speculating about Christ's return than we do serving Him. The point the angels were making to the disciples is that Jesus' return *is certain*. Thus we shouldn't waste time and energy worrying about when or whether Christ will return. Believe that He is coming again, on schedule, and stay focused on doing His business in the meantime.

Jesus left several instructions about what we should do while we await His return:

1. *Witness for Him everywhere you go.* Our Lord told His disciples to be His witnesses everywhere—even to the farthest ends of the earth (Acts 1:8).

2. *"Go into all the world and preach the gospel"* (Mark 16:15). This

command emphasizes the evangelistic and missionary nature of the church's ministry during the present era. We are to take the gospel to the whole world.

3. *"Repentance and remission of sins should be preached...to all nations"* (Luke 24:47). We're to call men and women to repent and believe the gospel.

4. *"Make disciples of all the nations, baptizing them"* (Matthew 28:19). Making converts and discipling them in their walk with God is a major emphasis of the church's mission.

5. *Continue building the church in every generation.* Jesus told His disciples that He would build His church with such power that "the gates of hell shall not prevail against it" (Matthew 16:18 KJV). Jesus pictured the church being on the march until He calls her home.

6. *"Occupy till I come"* (Luke 19:13 KJV), Jesus said in the parable of the talents. In this parable, the servants were to put their master's money to work until the master returned. We are to stay busy about the Master's business until He returns.

7. *Remain faithful until He returns.* Our Lord concluded His prophetic message in the Olivet Discourse by reminding His disciples to continue in faithful and wise service even though He might be gone a long time (Matthew 24:45; 25:14-30).

In the meantime, we can live with our eyes looking to the skies, watching for Christ to come, and with our feet on the earth, working for Him until He comes. We are to balance *expectation* (the awareness Jesus could come at any moment) with *participation* (serving Him faithfully until He comes). Living in the light of His coming keeps us focused on what is really important in life.

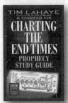

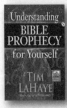